BALANCING

PREGNANCY

AND

WORK

BALANCING
PREGNANCY
AND
WORK

*How to Make the Most
of the Next 9 Months
on the Job*

NANCY W. HALL

A Stonesong Press Book

RODALE

© 2004 by Stonesong Press, LLC and Nancy W. Hall

Printed in the United States of America

Rodale Inc. makes every effort to use acid-free ∞, recycled paper ♻.

Book design by Joanna Williams

Library of Congress Cataloging-in-Publication Data

Hall, Nancy Wilson.
    Balancing pregnancy and work : how to make the most of the next 9 months on the job / Nancy W. Hall.
       p.   cm.
    Includes bibliographical references and index.
    ISBN 1–57954–787–7 paperback
    1. Pregnancy. 2. Pregnant women—Employment. I. Title.
    RG525.H239 2004
    618.2'4—dc22   2003022513

Distributed to the book trade by St. Martin's Press

2 4 6 8 10 9 7 5 3 1   paperback

A Stonesong Press Book

For David,
and for Wilson and Meg,
who keep me balanced

CONTENTS

GREAT BEGINNINGS

Susannah is a 27-year-old social worker for the state of North Carolina who has just begun to think seriously about getting pregnant for the first time. While she and her husband Jack, a freelance sports writer, have often talked about starting a family, those discussions always had a kind of dreamlike quality. But now Susannah finds herself thinking about the very practical issues of having a baby: How motherhood will affect her career. How much time she'll be able to take off from work. Money is tight already, and taking an unpaid maternity leave could make matters worse. Also, she worries about leaving her clients for very long. And she wonders if Jack, who works mainly from home, will be able to handle baby care and writing, or if they'll need to find affordable child care? Maybe it would be more practical to wait another year or two, but when she holds her girlfriend's 3-month-old daughter and gazes at the infant's wide eyes and tiny nose, inhaling her milky, powdery baby scent, all Susannah can think about is getting pregnant as soon as possible.

Thirty-four-year-old Arline, an airline ticket agent, and her 40-year-old husband Dell, a building contractor, have been trying to conceive for about 8 months. They're frustrated that they haven't *had any success yet, but Arline's doctor is encouraging. She tells them that 8 months isn't long at all, and urges them to relax, enjoy their attempts at baby-making, and use the time to make plans for balancing parenting and working once Arline does get pregnant.*

Kim, a 32-year-old hospice nurse, is enjoying the early days of her pregnancy. Only her boyfriend, her mother, and her closest friend know that she's pregnant, and she doesn't plan to tell her boss for several more months. Although she feels a bit guilty for not telling, and sometimes feels as if she's bursting to tell her friends at work, she knows that this time of having the sweet secret all to herself will never come again, and she wants to savor every minute. She loves this time of treasuring the mysterious life within her, of wondering what sort of mother she'll be. Sometimes she wonders how she'll be able to care for the baby and her patients as well, but then she realizes she still has months before she has to arrive at an arrangement that works for everyone.

YOUR TURN

Since you're reading this book, you're probably at a stage similar to Susannah, Arline, or Kim. Your dream baby may still be at the "gleam in your eye" stage, blessed with every possibility. Or you may be actively trying to conceive, already thinking of yourself as a mother-to-be. Or you may be pregnant already. If so, congratulations!

Just as no two pregnancies are alike, no two women, or couples, think about their growing family in the same way. Maybe you've planned for this baby ever since you were a little girl cradling your dolls, and you've been secretly reading pregnancy and baby care books for years. Maybe you never gave motherhood much thought, or had mixed feelings about the impact parenthood would have on your life. Maybe your pregnancy came as a surprise, and you are still trying to sort out your own feelings about the changes to come. Perhaps it's your first pregnancy, and much of what lies ahead seems mysterious and a little scary. Or it's your fifth, and you wonder whether your income and sanity will stretch along with your heart to accommodate another addition to your family. Or maybe you're awaiting the call that will tell you the baby you've longed to adopt is on the way, and it's time to make last-minute arrangements at home and at work.

If you're reading this book, chances are you have a job beyond mothering. You may work for yourself or someone else, in or out of your home, or you may be searching for a job. As a working woman and a mother-to-be, you are not alone. Nearly two-thirds of women in the United States with a child under age one are in the paid labor force. Reading this book is just as important as eating right and taking care of yourself during your pregnancy. The latter two protect you and your baby; this book will help protect your job and career.

GETTING A HEAD START ON PREGNANCY

If you're not pregnant yet, and you're reading this book because you're super organized, good for you. There are things you can do during this period (besides the obvious baby-making stuff—you're on your own there) to lay the groundwork for both a healthy pregnancy and a smooth transition from work to maternity leave and back to your job again.

Hopefully, by now, you've already seen your doctor and begun a pre-pregnancy program. This should include the following steps.

Build a healthful diet. Now is the time to curb any junk food habits and build a diet based on fruits, vegetables, dairy products,

3

Every Mother Is a Working Mother

It's a cliché, of course, to say that every mother is a working mother, but one that you might not have paid much attention to or taken to heart until you found out you were pregnant or decided to try for a baby. Yet one of the first things you'll often hear when you announce your pregnancy is: "Oh, are you going to keep working?"

On the other hand, no one ever asks a father-to-be whether *he's* going to keep his job after the baby comes. So let's start by setting out a few basic assumptions that form the underlying philosophy of this book.

Every mother is a working mother. In spite of its many rewards and its unparalleled importance, raising a child is the most difficult job on earth. Parenting is hard, never-ending (even when you're in your "official" workplace), and typically brings no pay and few material benefits. Thus, the phrase "working mother" is redundant.

Work/family issues are as much the concern of fathers as of mothers. This book is targeted largely at women because we are the ones who carry and nurse our babies. We are also the ones who have far too often found ourselves lacking the legal, social, and political support we need when trying to balance work and pregnancy. But fathers love, nurture, and care for their children just as we do. And sometimes, it may be fathers who get no respect in the parenting world.

Women are in the paid labor force for the same reasons men are: to feed, clothe, house, and protect our families, and to gain a sense of personal accomplishment for work well done. According to the New York-based Families and Work Institute, 55 percent of women with paid jobs provide more than half of their family's income. Almost half of these women who have children under age 3 are their family's sole breadwinner.

Child care is not a substitute for parental care. Supplemental child care is a fact of life for most American families. But the care arrangements families make, even when both parents work outside the home, should not interrupt, interfere with, or in any way supplant the love and care of the child's parents for her, nor of the child for the parents.

lean meats, and whole grains. Talk with your health care provider about which kinds of fish are safe for you; many contain unhealthy levels of mercury. If you're a vegetarian or have other dietary sensitivities or restrictions (lactose intolerance, for example), your doctor or midwife can help you to identify alternative healthy sources of protein or calcium.

Pop a prenatal vitamin. You'll need a prescription from your health care provider for this vitamin, but it's important. Numerous studies find that the folic acid in these vitamins (essential for cell reproduction and growth and also found in leafy vegetables, grains, breads, cereals, and liver, where it is known as folate) can help to prevent neural tube defects like spina bifida. Even though you may be eating a healthy diet, the additional nutritional insurance can't hurt. And the extra calcium in the prenatal vitamin can contribute to healthy bones—yours and the baby's!

Quit smoking. You probably already know how bad smoking is for you, but you should also be aware of the potential dangers should you become pregnant. Smoking increases your risk of having a tubal (ectopic) pregnancy, of miscarriage, and of premature delivery. Infants born to smokers are more likely to be of low birth weight, to have respiratory problems, and to die of Sudden Infant Death Syndrome (SIDS). Further, recent studies show that the effects of smoking during pregnancy may extend well into your child's life: Children born to women who smoke are more likely to be colicky as infants, and to have behavior problems as toddlers.

Trying to conceive? Then there are even more reasons to quit: Smoking can impair fertility by causing a decrease in estrogen. Smoking has also been linked to premature degeneration of the ovaries and depletion of healthy egg cells.

Limiting your exposure to second-hand smoke is important as

well. Second-hand smoke is associated with the same types of health risks as if you were the smoker—both for you, and when you get pregnant, for your baby.

Visit your doctor for a complete checkup. This should include a Pap test and gynecological exam, family medical history, and a screen for sexually transmitted diseases. Make sure your vaccinations are up to date. Blood tests should include a test for the presence of rubella antibodies (indicating that you've had or been inoculated against German measles, which can cause serious birth defects if you contract it during pregnancy), and a determination of whether you and your partner are Rh compatible (if not, you and your baby could have blood incompatibilities that could cause serious health complications for both of you, as well as for later babies).

Get a complete dental exam and teeth cleaning. By doing so, you'll avoid the need for dental x-rays during your pregnancy. Hormonal changes during pregnancy also make you more prone to gingivitis and periodontal disease, so starting with a clean slate—and clean teeth and gums—is a good idea.

Become familiar with your own menstrual cycle. If you're uncertain about how regular you are, or if your periods tend to arrive somewhat haphazardly, start charting their arrival on a calendar. This can help you to identify your most fertile times, and may serve as a clue for your health care provider in the event you have difficulty becoming pregnant (and help you pinpoint the date when you *do* become pregnant).

A HEALTHY BEGINNING

Since you're reading this book, chances are you're pregnant. If so, you've probably already seen your health care provider. It's important to call your obstetrician or midwife as soon as you know you're pregnant so the two of you can ensure you and your baby begin on the healthiest path possible. As long as you are basically healthy and not experiencing bleeding, spotting, or other problems, you'll likely be asked to come in for your first prenatal exam sometime between your 8th and 12th week of pregnancy.

Getting good care early on is important, because you want to make sure you start on a good prenatal vitamin (if you aren't already taking one), which is essential for both your and your baby's health. It's also important that the person who will be providing your health care during your pregnancy—and possibly delivering your baby—gets an overall picture of you and your health.

During that first visit, expect to describe your family history and receive a complete physical examination. This visit usually covers not just the physiological aspects of your health—weight, blood pressure, medical history—but also discussions of your lifestyle: demands of your job, nutritional habits, whether you drink, smoke, or use any recreational drugs, whether you exercise, and any potential hazards to which you could be exposed—as well as the health and general family history of the baby's father.

You'll also want to talk with your health care provider about prenatal tests that might be required for you and your child. Which—if any—prenatal screening or assessment tools you want to use during your pregnancy is a matter for you, your partner, and your healthcare provider to decide. Many factors, including your age, reproductive history, family history, and ethnicity, are taken into consideration when determining whether a certain test is right for you. Think of these tests as tools to help you control—or at least be aware of—the many elements that will characterize your pregnancy.

Testing, Testing . . .

Here's a brief guide to some of the most common prenatal tests currently available, who should get them, and when.

What: Multiple marker screening
Why: Down's syndrome, neural tube defects, other chromosomal disorders
Who: Nearly all pregnant women
How: Blood test
When: 15–18 weeks
Other: About 5 percent of tests result in false positive readings. The test detects about 66 percent of babies with Down's syndrome. If Down's is suspected, your doctor may suggest you follow up with an amniocentesis.

What: Amniocentesis
Why: Down's syndrome, trisomy 18, and other chromosomal disorders; determining gender
Who: Women 35 and older, women following up on an abnormal reading on the multiple marker screening, women with a family history of Down's syndrome or other genetically carried disease
How: A sample of amniotic fluid is withdrawn from the sac around the baby using a long, thin needle inserted through the abdomen and guided by ultrasound.
When: 15–18 weeks
Other: May be uncomfortable; mild cramping and spotting. About one in 200 procedures results in miscarriage.

What: Glucose tolerance test
Why: Screens for gestational diabetes
Who: Nearly all pregnant women, particularly those over 30, those who are overweight, have had a very large baby before, or have a family history of diabetes
How: An hour after you drink a sugar solution, a blood sample is taken and your glucose levels are tested. A positive result may require further testing.
When: 24–28 weeks
Other: About 12–15 percent of tests result in false positive readings. Some women may feel nauseated for a brief time after drinking the solution.

What: Ultrasound

Why: Numerous reasons, including gauging fetal size and position, detecting or confirming multiple pregnancy, detecting or helping to confirm or rule out certain defects (like Down's syndrome or limb abnormalities), determining gender

Who: Nearly every pregnant woman

How: A slippery gel is spread over the belly, then an instrument called a transducer is rolled over the belly, sending sound waves into the uterus to depict the fetus. If you have an ultrasound very early in the pregnancy—perhaps to confirm the pregnancy—it may be done intravaginally with the probe inserted through your vagina. Don't worry; it's painless.

When: Throughout pregnancy, at different times for different reasons

Other: False positives are rare, but follow-up testing may be done if the ultrasound indicates any problems. The procedure itself is painless, but it may tickle, and the gel can feel cold. Because images are clearer if your bladder is full, you may be asked to drink a lot before the procedure, and you may be uncomfortable holding it in for a long time.

Be sure to tell the technician if you *don't* want to know the baby's gender, lest the beans be spilled. Finally, technicians with more experience and better training are more adept at detecting birth defects. If you are at high risk for such a problem, ask your sonographer whether she is a registered medical diagnostic sonographer.

What: Group B strep screening

Why: Group B strep is a bacterium that women may carry without danger to themselves, but which may be passed to babies during delivery. It may cause pneumonia, meningitis, or serious blood infections in newborns.

Who: All pregnant women

How: Painless swabs of the vagina and rectum

When: 35–37 weeks

Other: If you have a positive result, you'll be treated with antibiotics during or shortly before labor.

DATE PLANNING

These days, home pregnancy tests are so accurate that most can tell you if you're pregnant within a day or so of a missed period. Of course, once you get the confirmation, one of your first questions will likely be: "When will my baby be born?" Knowing your due date helps you begin planning for parental leave, and can provide a sense of the big picture when it comes to work-related issues and events. For instance, it will help you know if you'll be able to stay on the job long enough to speak at the conference for which your paper has already been accepted. If you'll be too far along to fly to the trade show you've been organizing. If you'll be returning to work during your company's busiest season, or if you can adjust your plans to avoid it or to get back to your desk in time to help out.

We talk about the 9 months of pregnancy, but health professionals think of a full-term pregnancy in terms of weeks or days. Human babies gestate for approximately 40 weeks, or 280 days. And even if you're sure you conceived this baby exactly midway through your cycle, on the 14th day of the 28-day calendar on which menstruation typically operates, your health care provider measures it somewhat differently. To calculate your due date—or, in the quaint but slightly forbidding terms of a previous generation, your "estimated date of confinement," or EDC—the way your doctor does, get out your calendar. Figure out the first day of your last normal period and add 280 days. Presto! You have a date on which you could be giving birthday parties for many, many years.

If doing the math seems like too much trouble, figure out the first date of your last period and try one of the following online pregnancy calculators:

∗ www.4woman.gov/pregnancy/duedate1.cfm

∗ www.maternitymall.com/HomePregnancyCalculator.asp

∗ www.parentsplace.com/pregnancy/calculator

Of course, a baby considered to be full term rarely arrives smack on the 280th day of his or her gestation. On average, a full-term baby is one born at any time within a 5-week window starting 3 weeks prior to the due date (37 weeks) and ending 2 weeks after the due date (42 weeks). Your menstrual history provides some clue as to where your delivery might fall within this range. If your periods arrive every 28 days like clockwork, you're likely to deliver near your estimated due date. Women with shorter cycles tend to deliver slightly earlier, while women with longer cycles usually have slightly longer pregnancies. In general, though, there are no guarantees.

TO TELL OR NOT TO TELL

All too often, a pregnant woman is treated as if every aspect of her life—what she eats and drinks, how she feels, even how she looks—is subject to the same intensity of review as a Supreme Court decision. Before you can say "baby booties," your friends, family, and a host of complete strangers on trains and elevators, in the grocery store and at the office water-cooler offer their unsolicited advice. They tell you how and what to eat (or not to eat), how much to drink, and, of course, pat your swelling belly and comment on your weight, your skin, and your clothing in a manner Emily Post would have simply called rude.

Many women enjoy being the center of attention. Ellen, a real estate agent who gave birth to her first child when she was 31, loved it. "It made me feel really connected with the world. Sure, it was annoying sometimes, and occasionally I felt like my personal space was being violated a little too often, but mostly it was lovely that people seemed to care so much. A month or so after my son was born, I went to the market by myself for the first time since I'd delivered and not one person had a smile or a piece of unsolicited advice or a compliment for me—I'd become invisible again, and it was so sad! I say, enjoy it while it lasts."

But other women cringe at becoming such a public spectacle, and want to delay sharing the news for as long as possible. There are several good reasons to hold off on telling the world the minute you find out you're pregnant. For one, the majority of miscarriages occur in the first trimester of pregnancy, although the greatest risk passes by about the 14th week of pregnancy. If you keep the pregnancy between you and your partner and, heaven forbid, anything goes wrong, you won't have gotten everyone all excited. Of course, the downside to holding off is that *if* something goes wrong, you're going to need support and comfort; now you have to tell the people in your life about the pregnancy and the miscarriage all at once.

Then there's the issue of your job. It's inevitable that once people find out you're pregnant, they'll view you in a different way. The longer you wait, the less time you have to endure this. Also, becoming the "public property" pregnant women seem to turn in to can seem particularly inappropriate at the workplace. This is a place where you want to be valued for your brains, creativity, communication, and competence, not the size of your belly. You may also worry about losing your job or a promotion if your boss finds out you're pregnant. (Fortunately, the law says you cannot be fired or passed over for a promotion simply because you're pregnant, but I'll discuss that further in chapter 2.)

One reason to consider telling your boss earlier in your pregnancy is if your working conditions—standing all day, contact with toxins or other unhealthy environmental hazards—could harm you or the baby. I'll discuss this in detail in chapters 3 and 7.

Another reason to hold off on the telling is to give you and your partner time to get used to the idea of a baby. After all, few things will change your life as much as a child. Once you get over the initial shock, the fear may hit. About finances. Work. Your skills as a parent. It's much easier to work through some of those issues without the rest of the world interfering.

Plus, as teachers Beth and Jean-Paul discovered, having this "secret" between the two of you can bring you even closer as a couple. Both in their late thirties, the couple had been trying to conceive for so long that, as Beth noted, "Our friends had rather tactfully quit asking us about how the baby-making was going." So they found it remarkably easy to keep the pregnancy a secret for the first 8 weeks. "Those were just wonderful days—we felt closer than ever, and Jean-Paul was so attentive and caring," recalls Beth. "And, of course, the fact that sex was just for fun again, with no worries about contraception, and no fuss over when I was ovulating, just added spice to what was already a great time for us. Somehow, knowing that we'd never again be completely alone together, just the two of us, made it feel even more precious."

If, however, you're ready to shoot an e-mail to everyone in your address book, peek ahead to chapter 3, where I discuss the best ways to tell.

DREAM PLANNING: THE ULTIMATE PREGNANCY AND FAMILY LEAVE

Before you start talking to the folks at work about your good news, sit down and really think about what you want. The following exercise will help you clarify your own expectations of your pregnancy, family leave, and eventual return to work. Use these questions as starting points to help you envision what you really want from your time off, and how you see your life once you are both working and parenting.

✳ Picture your time off after the birth of your baby. What are you most looking forward to: time away from work, or time with the baby?

✳ Do you want to work until your water breaks, or would you love to take a few days or weeks before your due date to organize the baby's room, rest up for the impending labor and delivery, and spend some couple time with your partner?

✳ Do you pine to stay home with your baby until he or she is off to kindergarten? Or college? Or do you fantasize about getting back to work as soon as possible?

✳ What ideas/fantasies/fears/worries do you have about child care? Do you envision sharing baby care with your favorite sister, the retired woman across the street, or a fabulous on-site day care center you're sure your boss will authorize the company to build as soon as she hears your big news?

✳ How do you plan to nurture your couple relationship after the baby? How will you balance the demands of your respective jobs *and* the new baby *and* still have time and attention for each other?

✳ Consider what your husband or partner wants as well, and how he envisions early parenthood. Was your husband nurtured on *Leave It to Beaver*, a spotless home, and dinner on the table every night at 6:30 on the dot? Or *Malcolm in the Middle*, a comfortable level of chaos, and a catch-as-catch-can schedule? Is your partner's first priority keeping the family's financial ship floating as high as possible, or spending as much time as possible getting to know the new baby?

Or both? Now is the time to find out. Give your partner some time to think over the questions above, then discuss them with each other.

In talking together about your answers to the above questions, see if you can identify certain themes. If either of you dreams about a close bonding with the new baby, making time to be together in the first weeks and months may be a high-enough priority that it's worth taking as much leave time as you can get—even if you have to live lean for a while. If one of you has more of a my-home-is-my-well-mortgaged-castle movie playing in your head, establishing a sense of financial security may be essential to enjoying your time off.

The same goes if you're in a "bring-home-the-bacon, fry-it-up-in- the-pan" mode. Maybe you're already itching to get to the thrill of the balancing act.

Knowing what you both desire will help you juggle your interests as a parent with your job-related interests and needs, as well as the needs of the relationship you share.

WHEN YOU'RE ON DIFFERENT PAGES

Of course, this discussion could be quite eye opening, and you may discover that the two of you have very different ideas about parenthood, work, and balancing the two areas. Now is certainly a better time to talk about these issues than the night before your parental leave runs out. For instance, consider the case of Elizabeth and her husband, Bill. Elizabeth, 35, spent much of her first trimester lost in a dream of how lovely the early weeks with her first baby were going to be. She enjoyed her job as a court stenographer, and looked forward to returning to work, but hoped to be able to stretch out the 12 weeks of family leave she'd be getting by taking 8 full weeks off and working part-time for another 8 weeks. It never occurred to her that Bill, a school librarian, wasn't on the same wavelength. A casual discussion about child care a few weeks before their baby was born revealed that he assumed she'd be returning to work after just a month or 6 weeks. Both Elizabeth and Bill were taken aback at how far apart their visions were. They were both angry, too—she at what she perceived as his insensitivity to her needs, he at her apparent lack of concern for financial matters.

Such misunderstandings can lead to horrendous fights just as you're returning to work, with misunderstandings galore because you're both probably exhausted. So a fight over who will clean the cat litter box turns out to *really* be about how upset he is that you're going back to work when *his* mother stayed home until he was a freshman in college. Or you may hear yourself saying that you don't think he loves the baby as much as you do, but your *real* concern is that the wonderful woman who's coming in the morning to take care of your little one while you head back to work is really a serial killer/kidnapper/drug addict.

Honest—these are the things new parents fight about when what they're *really* worried about is whether they'll be good parents. If you understand each other's basic feelings about how to balance work and family issues now, while you can still fit into your regular-sized jeans, you won't entirely eliminate these little crises, but you'll be closer to understanding each others' *real* fears and priorities so you can sort them out together before they become catastrophes.

If, like Elizabeth and Bill, you find yourselves in opposite corners, try taking each other's perspectives and examining each other's motives. Eventually, Bill and Elizabeth realized that the bottom line for both of them was the baby's welfare and the stability of the family. Once they examined all of their family leave options (as chapter 2 of this book will help you to do, too), they were able to make the compromises that satisfied both of them.

HEALTH INSURANCE COVERAGE

Before you make any decisions about what type of leave you'd like to take, you'll also need to consider your health insurance coverage. Remember that your company is not required by law to offer health insurance, but if it does, it *is* required to continue to provide the same health coverage while you're on FMLA leave.

That doesn't mean, however, that your health insurance will automatically cover your pregnancy. Some policies don't cover pregnancies. Some won't cover you if you became pregnant before your policy went into effect, which is what's known as a "pre-existing condition." Again, you may not be able to control your insurance situation, but you can make sure that you have fully grasped the situation before making a plan and sharing it with others at your workplace.

If you are not covered by employer-supported insurance, perhaps your spouse is. (If you choose this option, be aware that you can't be denied coverage for a pre-existing condition if you're simply moving from your group plan to his.) If you find yourself without any health insurance during your pregnancy and leave of absence, check with your state's Department of Social Services or Department of Health Care Access to see if there are other options, such as Medicaid or low-cost insurance plans that might help. You could also work with your obstetrician's office to identify low-cost alternatives to private health insurance in your area, and talk to an insurance broker, who should have information on plans for which you might qualify.

FINANCIAL PLANNING

Next, sit down and do some basic calculations regarding your family budget. Appendix C on page 239 contains a detailed worksheet to help you list everything that comes in and goes out in a typical month. First, list all sources of income, including any rental income, alimony, child support, or other non-job-related payments. Now figure out—very approximately—monthly expenses. If you already track your finances on a computer program like Quicken, this should be easy. If not, complete part II of the worksheet. As you fill in the information, be sure to include those spur-of-the-moment purchases, such as newspapers and Starbucks coffee, that you might not usually think about but that can quickly add up. Now figure out how these expenses will change if you take family leave. Base the change in income on who will take leave (you? your partner? both of you?) and for how long. If you have income from any source during this period, add it in the second column of part I; if your leave will be unpaid, subtract the entire cost of your job-related income. But also subtract job-related expenses, like clothing, transportation, parking, lunches out, and take-out dinners.

Next, fill in part III of the worksheet as best you can. If you don't have a good idea of what disposable diapers or onesies cost, now is a good time to survey some stores so you can make these figures as accurate as possible.

Finally, subtract your total for baby expenses and your total for general expenses during leave from your total income during this time. Your goal is to arrive at a reasonable ballpark estimate of how taking unpaid leave (or partially paid leave) will affect your family's bottom line.

Armed with this information about your finances and with some idea about the goals you have for your leave and subsequent work arrangements, you can take the next step—investigating family leave options. Knowing what you're entitled to is essential—both in terms of your rights at work and while you're on leave—and should, ideally, be well-established before you spread the joyful news at work. Chapter 2 covers this in detail and with plenty of real-life examples about how pregnancy-related laws like the Pregnancy Discrimination Act and the more recently enacted Family and Medical Leave Act apply to you and your situation.

HERE AND NOW

So, back to the beginning. Congratulations. Whether you've just found out you're pregnant, or you've just made the decision to start trying, you're entering a new world, a wonderful world filled with joy (as well as numerous challenges, excitements, frustrations, heartaches, and unexpected delights). Savor this time. The beginning of your pregnancy is one of the most important periods of the entire 9 months. Remember that you're at the very start of what will be a very long path.

I can promise you this: The tools in this book will help you find a way to balance the demands and rewards of pregnancy and work. In the coming chapters, you'll learn about your legal rights as a pregnant woman, how to break the happy news to friends and family, workplace hazards you should be aware of—and what to do about them. I'll tell you how to cope with nausea and fatigue on the job, what to wear to retain a professional image as your stomach swells to the size of a large watermelon, how to plan for your leave, find child care, and return to the workplace postpartum. Buckle up: You're starting on a wonderful journey.

KEYS TO KEEPING
THE BALANCE

If you're already pregnant, enjoy this amazing time when you, or you and your partner or husband, can treasure your special secret, enjoy your last few months as a childless couple, and dream about the ways your lives will change.

If you're planning a pregnancy, use this time to improve your health and have some basic medical screenings. Do everything you can now to have a healthy pregnancy—and a healthy baby later.

If you're pregnant now, schedule an appointment with your ob/gyn or midwife as early as possible to continue on the path to a healthy pregnancy.

Spend this time sorting out your feelings about parenthood, work, and the places in your lives where they intersect. Talk with your partner about your dreams and goals for your life together. But don't panic if you find your goals at odds with his. Talking about your conceptions of family, and, in particular, of how working fits into this picture, can help each of you to understand the other's point of view.

2

YOUR PREGNANCY,
YOUR JOB, YOUR RIGHTS

Charlotte had two radically different pregnancies, one when she was 26, the second 4 years later. She felt healthy throughout both pregnancies and delivered both babies easily with no medication. "I love both my kids," says Charlotte. "But I just felt completely different during my second pregnancy, because the second time around I didn't have to worry about having a job to return to. This reduced my stress level immeasurably!" Charlotte's son Ben was born in 1990, her daughter Graciela in 1994. The difference? Between the two pregnancies, the Family and Medical Leave Act, or FMLA, was signed into law, giving women who work for companies with 50 or more employees job-protected, 12-week leaves. This leave can be used to care for a family member's (or your own) illness or injury, or as a parental leave when you give birth, adopt a baby, or take in a foster child.

Before President Clinton signed the FMLA in 1993, the only protection pregnant women had on the job came through the Pregnancy Discrimination Act, or PDA. I'll go into the PDA in more detail on page 24, but it basically said you couldn't be fired because of your pregnancy. Nowhere did it guarantee you a comparable job after you had the baby, or any kind of leave—rights that most other developed nations provided at the time. That not only put the United States in an embarrassing position, but also may have actually harmed many of its newest citizens. Knowing they have a job to return to after giving birth or adopting a baby safeguards many families' economic stability, giving new parents time to provide their child with a strong start in life.

WHY FAMILY LEAVE MATTERS

The transition to parenthood, no matter how joyful, is one of the most stressful experiences you'll ever encounter. "The first time I took my new son for his first checkup, his doctor asked me whether motherhood was everything I expected," recalls Hannah, 31, a nurse at a geriatric care center. "I told him I was loving it, that it was way more fun than I'd expected it to be. But it was also so much harder! He's so tiny and helpless, he keeps weird hours, and he expects the milk bar to be open around the clock. And, of course, I was still recovering from labor and delivery even as a lot of my energy was going into nursing him. I don't know how I would have managed if I'd had to go back to work a couple of weeks after he was born. Besides, it would have broken my heart to leave him so soon."

Experts in developmental psychology and pediatrics agree that the first few months of life are uniquely important ones for parents and babies. Getting to know any new baby takes time—time spent together. Years ago, it was generally believed that babies are passive little creatures, just waiting around for us to mold them into fine, upstanding individuals. Now we know that each child is an active partner in the parent-child relationship from the moment of birth. We influence each other's behaviors, learning to read each other's signals through countless daily interactions—cuddling, playing, talking and responding, even bathing. In this way, a baby's cognitive and social development gets off to a solid start.

A strong beginning requires a stable, loving environment, particularly during the earliest weeks and months of life. Your baby needs to understand that the world is a predictable place, an understanding that depends largely on the kind of continuity and responsiveness a small number of consistently present caregivers provide.

The demands of the workplace, however, often come into conflict with what parents say they need during this time. Research conducted at Yale University showed that women who had to return to employment before they felt physically ready to be back at work or emotionally ready to leave their babies in the care of others reported feeling stressed, guilty, and cheated out of an important and irreplaceable experience.

This doesn't mean that going back to work earlier than you want to or leaving your baby with a loving caregiver will wreak havoc on your child's future happiness and competence. But it does mean that, given a choice between being able to be with your baby during the earliest weeks, months, or years of her life, and being forced to return to your desk full time before she's a month old (as was often the case in the parental dark ages before 1993), it's much better for everyone if you can be with her.

HOW THE OTHER HALF LIVES

In other industrialized nations, the demands of the workplace are better balanced with those of family life. If you live and work in Canada, Italy, Norway, or Sweden, for instance, your employee benefits probably allow you to be home with your baby often enough and long enough so that your relationship becomes smooth and predictable, secure and comfortable. (See "Parental Leaves around the

World" below.) In many countries, the right to take child-related leave extends to the parents of older children, too, enabling them to take time off to attend school events and parent-teacher meetings. More than three-quarters of developed nations around the world have national leave policies for new mothers. Even better, parents in most of these nations continue to get paid while on leave.

THE PREGNANCY DISCRIMINATION ACT

Before we talk about the Family and Medical Leave Act, let's go back a few years and examine its precursor (which is still very much

Parental Leaves around the World

Here is just a sample of how the United States stacks up against other countries when it comes to government-supported parental leaves.

Nation	Time Off	Percent Income Replacement*
Austria	16 weeks	100
Belgium	15 weeks	75–80
Canada	20 weeks	55
France	18 weeks	100
Germany	14 weeks	100
Italy	20 weeks	80
Luxembourg	16 weeks	100
Norway	1 year	80–100
Spain	16 weeks	100
Sweden	18 months	80
United States	12 weeks	None

* In some of the nations listed, a longer leave is available at a lower rate of income replacement. In Spain, for instance, parents can take 3 more months of pay at a flat rate, and 3 additional months without pay.

in effect): the Pregnancy Discrimination Act. This 1978 amendment to the Civil Rights Act of 1964 made (and continues to make) it illegal for any employer of 15 or more workers to treat a pregnant employee differently than a non-pregnant employee. Bottom line? *You cannot be fired for being pregnant.*

Other provisions of the PDA prevent discrimination on the basis of pregnancy in hiring. Should you find yourself job-hunting while pregnant (something we'll talk more about in chapter 3), know that it is illegal for a prospective employer to give you anything less than the same consideration she would give to a comparably qualified but non-pregnant candidate for the same job. This, of course, can be notoriously difficult to enforce.

When Sarah, a 33-year-old freelance graphic designer, applied for several part-time positions late in the second trimester of her pregnancy, she was turned down for every one. "The interviews all went so well," she says. "I thought I'd really clicked with the people I would have been working for, and they were impressed with my portfolio. In at least one case, I knew the artist who was eventually hired, and, frankly, I thought I'd have been a better match. I can't prove it, of course, but I do have a sneaking feeling that my being pregnant spooked them. I could really use at least one reliable source of income—not to mention some benefits—but at this point I'm so discouraged that I'm just going to enjoy the flexibility freelancing gives me and apply for a more conventional job when the baby is 6 months old."

The PDA also stipulates that your employer cannot require that you take leave because you're pregnant if you would not otherwise be asked to do so, as long as you can safely perform the duties your job requires. Additionally, it allows you to return to work as soon as you feel ready; your employer may not set a predetermined minimum leave time or ask you to stay out longer than you had planned. Because the PDA is based on the aspects of pregnancy that might lead it to be viewed as a physical disability, neither fathers nor parents of adopted babies are specifically covered.

Finally, the Pregnancy Discrimination Act says your employer must make the same reasonable accommodations for you on the job that he would make for any other employee, either male or female, with an illness or disability. If you're a tightrope walker at the circus, and the guy who gets shot out of the cannon was given a desk job for 6 weeks following back surgery, you're entitled to an alternative job under the Big Top until you're able to resume your feats of daring.

The PDA stood 27-year-old benefits manager Janice in good stead during her pregnancy. Janice, who worked for a religious publishing house, was a little nervous announcing her pregnancy at work. She and the baby's father had been living together quite happily for years, but they were not married, and her boss and fellow employees tended to take a rather dim view of single mothers. In fact, her boss was clearly disapproving when she told him her news, and his attitude didn't improve much throughout her pregnancy. He was savvy enough, however, not to let his beliefs affect his treatment of her on the job. He obeyed the law in every respect, but never went out of his way to inquire after her health or—after her return from maternity leave—that of her baby. Janice eventually left her job for a more congenial and supportive workplace; when she did, her boss gave her a positive and businesslike recommendation.

THE FAMILY AND MEDICAL LEAVE ACT

The Pregnancy Discrimination Act represented a big step for pregnant women, but it was only a first step. Although the PDA required employers to hold a job open for a pregnant woman for as long as

The Pregnancy Discrimination Act at a Glance

Here are the basic provisions of the PDA:

* It is illegal for an employer to treat pregnancy-related disabilities differently from other disabilities.

* An employer may not dismiss or refuse to hire a woman because she is pregnant.

* A woman may not be denied a promotion because she is pregnant.

* An employer may not require a woman to take maternity leave unrelated to her ability to work, as long as she is able to carry out the responsibilities of her job.

* An employer may not prevent a woman from returning to her job for a predetermined period of time following childbirth.

* When an employee takes maternity leave, her job must be held open for her if it would be held open for other employees taking disability leave.

* Reasonable adjustments to a pregnant woman's working environment or conditions must be made as needed; these might include seating, more bathroom breaks, and altered work hours.

* Employers are required to provide pregnant women with a harassment-free and non-discriminatory work environment.

* Pregnancy-related benefits and protections cannot be limited to married employees.

they would for a non-pregnant employee on leave for a physical disability, these safeguards were not fully spelled out in the form of job-protection guarantees. Pregnancy-related discrimination was also difficult to prove. Even after passage of the PDA, women continued to lose their jobs when they became mothers.

For years, scholars and politicians debated whether a federally sanctioned job-protected family leave would ever be a reality. Maternity leaves have historically been linked to disability leaves, so the notion that a new mother *or father* would be granted leave was as revolutionary as disposable diapers had been back in the 1960s. Several in-depth studies of how a federally-enforced parental leave policy might work emphasized not only how such policies would affect families, but also how they would affect businesses—particularly small ones.

The National Partnership for Women and Families (then known as the Women's Legal Defense Fund) and a multidisciplinary study group at the Yale University Bush Center for Child Development and Social Policy conducted intensive inquiries into balancing the needs of working families against those of employers. They both concluded that a national family leave policy would, in fact, be humane and good for families as well as be economically feasible—even advantageous—for employers. Their findings were instrumental in helping to shape the legislation that finally became the Family and Medical Leave Act, as were House Representatives Howard Berman, Patricia Schroeder, and William Clay, and Senator Christopher Dodd, who co-sponsored the original bill.

Several attempts to pass maternity leave legislation stronger than the PDA were struck down on the basis of sex discrimination, since the proposed legislation targeted only women. The first drafts of bills calling for parental (not just maternal) leave legislation appeared in the early 1980s. Some of these never made it out of their Congressional committees.

Even when the FMLA finally came up for debate in both houses of Congress in 1987, agreement about how to pass such legislation was controversial. Business lobbies, particularly those representing small businesses, predicted serious negative outcomes from the passage of such a law. Opponents of government involvement in the lives of families objected to the legislation on the grounds that it amounted to telling parents how to raise their children. Liberal forces argued that the proposed law, with its 12 weeks of unpaid leave, was a good start, but not adequate to meet the needs of parents who needed more time off and income replacement during the leave.

Congress passed the FMLA in 1990. Then-President George H. Bush vetoed the legislation, saying that it was not in the best interests of business. Both houses passed it again in 1992; again, President Bush vetoed family leave. In 1993, the legislation was passed for the third time. This time, newly inaugurated President Clinton signed the bill into law. In his remarks at the signing ceremony, he affirmed the right and responsibility of parents to spend this important time with their young children. President Clinton also emphasized the significant role of the federal government in making this opportunity possible.

The basic provisions of the FMLA are fairly straightforward. Your job—or, under certain circumstances, a comparable job with equal pay and benefits—will be protected while you take leave:

* If you are having a baby or your spouse is having a baby
* If you are adopting a baby or taking in a foster child
* If you are caring for a child, parent, or spouse with a serious health condition
* If you yourself have a serious health condition
* For up to 12 weeks in any year

As you can see, the FMLA applies to fathers as well as mothers, making the United States among the 9 percent of countries worldwide that offers parental leave to both parents. Additionally, you are covered under the provisions of FMLA if each of the following conditions is met:

✳ Your employer has had 50 or more employees on the payroll, working within 75 miles of your work site, for at least 20 work weeks during the current or previous year

✳ You have worked for your employer for at least 12 months and have worked at least 1,250 hours during the previous year

During your job-protected leave:

✳ Your employer is not obligated by law to pay you, although some employers may provide some pay through disability insurance programs.

✳ If your employer pays for all or a portion of your health insurance coverage, he or she must continue to do so during your leave; you may be required to continue to pay whatever you normally pay for such coverage.

The FMLA works best when employers and employees work together. Bev, 37, a translator for a multinational consulting firm, knew her boss wouldn't be thrilled that she was taking 12 weeks of leave when she and her husband adopted a little boy from Colombia. "He was pretty unhappy, because my job is so specialized, and I'm good at what I do. And he's a good guy. I felt bad that it was going to put him in a bind for me to be gone." In the old, pre-FMLA days, she said, he might have just replaced her, which would have meant hiring someone who had no relationship with the regular clients.

In the end, Bev and her boss compromised. She agreed to come to the office one day a week beginning the fifth week of her leave, and work on written translations from home as time permitted. In exchange, her boss agreed to pay for the baby and Bev's nanny to accompany her on some overseas business trips after she returned to work. "I know that under the law I didn't have to make these concessions," says Bev, "and neither did he. But I love my baby *and* my job, and in the end this made things work better for both of us."

In fact, 10 years after the FMLA went into effect, both employers and employees say it's making things better—on both sides.

* Employees need and take advantage of family leave: 20 million have taken leave under FMLA since it became law.

* Employers say dealing with the administrative details of FMLA is easier and less costly than they'd anticipated; more than 90 percent called the regulations "very easy" to comply with.

* About 9 out of 10 businesses reported no or only small cost increases; and, contrary to predictions, smaller businesses had a somewhat easier and less costly time implementing FMLA than did larger businesses.

* Many larger firms actually reported cost savings related to FMLA, mostly from reduced employee turnover and training, and increased productivity and morale.

While the FMLA is certainly a step in the right direction, it is just that, a step. There's still a far road to be traveled. Most important: The vast majority of parents who take leave under FMLA don't get paid. FMLA does not mandate that employers continue to pay employees on leave, so most don't.

Depressed? We should be. We should all be out rioting in the streets, or at least writing reams of protest letters. But since it's difficult enough for most of us to balance work, pregnancy, child care, and picking out wallpaper for the nursery, protesting a law that's way better than anything our mothers had probably isn't high on most of our priority lists.

(continued on page 34)

Is Your Company Family-Friendly?

Nearly 30 percent of 6,800 parents responding to a BabyCenter.com survey in 2002 said they worked for a family-friendly company. An additional 35 percent described their employer as somewhat family friendly. What does this mean?

Family-friendly companies typically provide a range of benefits intended to make it more convenient or affordable for parents to balance the demands of working and parenting. These may range from basic benefits like flexible spending accounts for health care and child care to more generous family leaves than those mandated by law, to on-site or subsidized high-quality child care, to truly wonderful luxuries like prepared family dinners available for purchase, or dry-cleaning pick up and drop off at work.

If you want to see how your company stacks up against others before putting gentle pressure on your employer to offer more parent-oriented benefits, take a look at the annual index of the 100 best companies for working moms in *Working Mother* magazine's October issue. In 2003, the top 10 companies in its index were (in alphabetical order):

* Abbott Laboratories: pharmaceuticals and biotech

* Booz Allen Hamilton: financial and professional services

* Bristol-Myers Squibb: pharmaceuticals and biotech

* Eli Lilly: pharmaceuticals and biotech

* Fannie Mae: secondary mortgage lender

* General Mills: manufacturer of cereals and other food products

* IBM: information technologies

* Prudential Financial, Inc.: financial and professional services

* S. C. Johnson and Sons: household products manufacturer

* Wachovia Corporation: banking

Family-friendly benefits offered by these companies included on-site child care, mentoring programs, flexible work arrangements, management training in work/life issues, paid leave for some employees, and a commitment to move more women into managerial positions. Entry-level workers at these companies receive the same access to great benefits as upper-level management.

How can you get your own company to offer more compassionate policies?

* First, do your homework. Knowing what competing companies within your industry offer—and how these policies improve their bottom line—is essential legwork.

* Second, ask. "What sort of day care subsidies does Grommet World offer? None? Really? I wonder what it would take to get a policy like that of our chief competitor implemented here?"

* Gather support. Ask around—preferably without appearing to be stirring up a mutiny—and try to gauge the level of demand for the policy or policies you have in mind.

* Approach the right person. If your company is small or your position is high, you're better placed to speak with a supervisor about your wish list. If you're part of a collective bargaining agreement, talk to your union representative.

* Don't give up when the answer is "no." It may take a long time to plant the seed about a family-friendly policy, but eventually a groundswell of support for the idea will grow, and responsive management may then be more willing to consider your concerns.

Family-friendly companies aren't offering these benefits out of the goodness of their hearts. They're just running a smart business. Management surveys consistently show that keeping employees happy with family-friendly benefits and policies reduces employee turnover and training/orientation costs, and improves employee morale and productivity. The University of Michigan School of Business, through its American Customer Satisfaction Index, found that companies who offer family-friendly policies have higher customer satisfaction ratings, and that these, in turn, are typically correlated with higher stock values. So maybe it's true what they say: If mama's happy, *everybody's* happy!

Later, when you're a more experienced parent, you can lobby your Congressional representatives during that free time you have between sucking the playground dirt off your kid's pacifier and figuring out whether the tomato sauce on a slice of pizza counts as a vegetable.

HOW DOES THE FMLA APPLY TO *MY* JOB?

The basic provisions of the Family and Medical Leave Act are fairly straightforward: what's offered, who's covered, and who's not. But, as with any self-respecting government regulation, the devil is in the details. Spelling out the intricacies of how the FMLA applies to each person's unique situation is beyond the scope of this book, but here are answers to some of the most frequently asked questions about FMLA coverage.

Can my husband and I each take 12 weeks off?

Either parent, or both parents, can take leave under FMLA for the birth or adoption of a baby, to bring a foster child into the home, to care for a seriously ill child or other family member, or for your own serious medical condition, including pregnancy complications. There are some exceptions, however. When Janelle and Stuart were planning their family leave, they were disappointed to discover that they were eligible for only 12 weeks of leave between them: If Stuart wanted to take 2 weeks off immediately following their baby's birth, Janelle would be able to take only 10 weeks. The reason? Both are employed by the same software design corporation. The regulation that gives parents who work for the same employer a combined total of 12 weeks of leave instead of 12 weeks each was designed to limit the burden on the employer.

34

When I tell my employer about my need to take leave, I'll only have been working for the company for 10 months, but my leave won't begin for 4 more months—am I still eligible for a job-protected leave?

Yes. You only have to have worked 12 months for your employer by the time your leave begins.

How much time can I take off?

The FMLA guarantees eligible employees up to a total of 12 work weeks of leave during any 12-month period. Your employer can chose any of several definitions of "12-month period"— using the calendar year, the fiscal year, the year as defined by the date on which you were hired, the previous 12 months, a 12-month period beginning on the first date of your leave, or a 12-month period consistent with the employer's work year.

Susan Fisher, 40, a department store buyer in New York City, took 10 weeks off for the birth of her daughter. Six months later,

The Horse's Mouth: When You Need the Details

A simple, user-friendly edition of the FMLA can be found on the Web site of the National Partnership for Women and Families: www.nationalpartnership.org.

For very specific questions about how the FMLA is applied, however, it's better to go straight to the source. The complete text of the FMLA can be found on the federal Department of Labor's Web site: www.dol.gov. Look for "Family and Medical Leave Act" in the easy-to-access alphabetical index.

To inquire by phone about how the FMLA applies to you, call (800) 669-4000 for the number of the branch office nearest you, or check the government section (blue pages) of your local telephone book. Find your local office of the federal government's Department of Labor under "Labor Department."

when her mother was laid up following knee surgery, Susan was able to use the remaining 2 weeks to fly to Kentucky to care for her.

I work for a college that is closed every year for the week between Christmas and New Year's Day, and my leave will encompass this week. Does that mean I get an extra week off?

You must have been nice instead of naughty: Santa has indeed brought you an extra week off. If you are on leave during a period in which employees are not usually expected to report to work for 1 or more weeks because your company's business activities temporarily cease, these days don't count against your FMLA leave. If, on the other hand, a shorter holiday falls within your leave—July 4 or Labor Day, for instance— you are not entitled to an extra day as compensation.

When I went into premature labor in my 6th month, my doctor put me on bed rest. Fortunately, I delivered a healthy baby boy only 2 weeks early. I was stunned to discover, though, that by the time he was born, the company's take was that I'd already used up 9 weeks of the 12 weeks I'm entitled to under FMLA. I really don't want to go back to work in 3 weeks—is this legal?

Technically, yes. The leave you took to enable you to keep your job while you were on bed rest counts against your 12 weeks. In many cases, however, you can make a disability-based arrangement for some additional leave, though there is no guarantee that your job will be protected beyond the 12th week of your leave. Special cases like yours are typically covered on a case-by-case basis, taking into account what your employer offers, what your state offers, what your physician recommends, and how valuable you are as an employee. Get all the information you can, determine what you want to ask for in terms of additional leave, and figure out whether you and your employer can reach some kind of compromise.

When I come back to work, I'd like to ease back in by working only a few days a week, but that means it will take longer than 12 calendar weeks before I'm back full time. Do I lose any leave that I can't fit in within 12 calendar weeks?

No. It may help if you think of the leave available to you as 60 work days, rather than as 12 work weeks. FMLA permits employees to take intermittent leave. For example, Ellen, 34, works full-time as a bank teller and plans to work right up until the day she gives birth. She arranged to extend her leave after the baby is born by taking leave for 6 full weeks, then working 3 days a week for the equivalent of the remaining 6 weeks. You can find more detailed information about how best to negotiate such a schedule—or a comparable one in which you ease back into the workplace—in chapter 10.

Are my benefits protected while I'm on leave?

An employer who voluntarily provides coverage under a group health care plan for employees must continue to do so during your family leave. The coverage provided must be the equivalent of what would have been provided if you weren't on leave—for example, if your plan covers your whole family, or offers dental and eye care, it must continue to do so while you're on leave. You will be asked to continue to make any contribution to this health care coverage that you typically make. Other benefits—life insurance, a gym membership, the key to the executive washroom—are continued at the discretion of your employer.

What about the other benefits I get during a typical working month? Will I continue to accrue new vacation and sick time? And will my employer continue to make pension contributions or matching 401K contributions during my leave?

In most cases, no. Since you are considered not to be in service during your leave period, your employer will not be granting you new vacation and sick days (and remember, in most cases you have to use these up as part of your leave). For the same reason, your employer is not required to continue to make contributions to your pension or 401K plans during your leave. If, however, you work at one of those rare and golden companies that provides a fully or partially paid leave at this time, the employer may, at its discretion, continue to make such payments. If you're unsure, check with your human resources department.

I was next in line for a seniority-based promotion to supervisor at my office, but was bypassed because I'm pregnant and will be starting my family leave in 2 months. Is this legal?

Nope. The Pregnancy Discrimination Act clearly states that it is illegal to bypass an employee for a promotion because she is pregnant. The FMLA further says that you cannot be deprived of any seniority while on leave (though you don't continue to accrue seniority while you're out). You may want to bring this complaint to the attention of the office of the Equal Employment Opportunity Commission (EEOC) in your state. You can contact them by dialing (800) 669-4000.

I work for a company that's too small to be covered by FMLA. I've heard that individual states sometimes have their own family leave laws, though. If the federal government doesn't offer me leave, but my state does, who wins?

You do. When the FMLA was enacted, it set a minimum standard for parental leaves. States are permitted—but not required—to offer leaves that are more generous in terms of the amount of time offered and income replacement provided, and many of them do. If you are covered by these plans, you are entitled to whichever of the plans—the federal plan or the one offered by your state—is more generous. A number of states, in fact, offer coverage to parents who wouldn't be covered at all under FMLA, typically by lowering the

If You Think Your Rights Have Been Violated . . .

If you think all or some of your rights as an employee covered under the Family and Medical Leave Act and/or the Pregnancy Discrimination Act have been violated, you may file a complaint or get information by contacting the Equal Employment Opportunity Commission, which is a division of the Department of Labor. To do this, call (800) 669-4000. The Department of Labor will work with you to determine whether your complaint has merit, and what remedies might be offered. Similar information is also available online at http://www.eeoc.gov.

Typically, a complaint must be filed within 2 years of the action you believe violated your rights, though under certain circumstances this time period may be extended to three years. In general, the sooner you file your complaint, the sooner you can expect it to be addressed. Remedies for FMLA or PDA violations—that is, what you get if the Department of Labor finds your complaint is warranted—may include some or all of the following:

* Back pay as appropriate to the situation
* Benefits previously denied
* Other compensation in question
* Reinstatement of denied employment
* Reasonable attorney's fees and other court costs
* Other actions or compensations, depending on the nature of the complaint

number of employees a workplace must employ in order to be included under FMLA.

There are several ways to get the information you're looking for. Start by checking out the state-by-state data in Appendix B on page 236. Though the data was current at the time this book went to press, new legislation is always in the works to improve family leave coverage and eligibility at the state level, so be sure you confirm what's offered where you live. Other sources of information are:

 * The human resources or personnel office where you work
 * Your union representative, if you're covered under a collective bargaining agreement
 * Your local Department of Labor office, usually found in the government section of your telephone book (most often in the blue pages)
 * The Web pages of the National Partnership for Women and Families, which maintains an extensive, current, and user-friendly section on family leave legislation, including information on what policies individual states offer (www.nationalpartnership.org).

While I was on leave following the birth of my daughter, cute sleepers weren't the only things I got in pink: I got my pink slip 3 weeks before I'd planned to return to the office. Isn't my job protected while I'm on leave?

Yes, as long as a job exists to protect. If you believe you were laid off *because* of your pregnancy, you may file a complaint with the Department of Labor's EEOC as outlined above. If, however, economic circumstances force your employer to eliminate, say, a layer of management across the board, or an entire shift of workers, or to close a shop or office because a specific project was canceled, you can be laid off like anyone else. Should this happen, your employer also has the right to terminate coverage of your group health benefit (unless you are covered under a collective bargaining agreement that guarantees some continuation of coverage in the event of a layoff). You are, however, entitled to whatever severance benefits you would have received if you weren't on leave when the layoff occurred.

I want to take leave under FMLA but I don't want to tell my employer I'm pregnant, or share details of my impending delivery. Must I tell why I'm requesting leave?

Yes, the family leave legislation stipulates that you must state the reason for the leave. It's sufficient, though, to say you're expecting a baby and plan to be on leave for most of September, October, and part of November. It is not necessary to divulge intimate personal or medical details of your plan, and you do not have to provide medical records to your employer.

Does "job-protected leave" mean I'm guaranteed to get my old job back after my leave?

Job protection means you will either be given your old job back or an "equivalent position" in which the pay, benefits, and—to the extent possible—responsibilities will be the same as those in your previous job. For instance, Carol, 29, worked for a pharmaceuticals company evaluating experimental medical technologies. Because her duties required a Master's degree in pharmacology, the company was unable to find a temporary worker to take her place to finish a time-sensitive project, and so they hired a permanent replacement to continue Carol's work after her family leave began. When it was time for her to return, her boss worked with Carol to create a new position to match her skills. She now earns a slightly larger salary than in her previous position, coordinating the results of clinical drug trials on one of the company's products.

SPECIAL CASES

The broad provisions of FMLA don't apply equally well to all occupations. Teachers, for instance, typically work on a specialized calendar year, have their own set of breaks, and have clients (their students) who are unusually dependent upon them. There are, therefore, special rules guiding family leave for teachers and many other school staffers.

Several other employee groups have special issues relevant to family leave coverage, including:

Federal employees. If you are employed by the federal government, either as a civil servant or a congressional employee, you are covered under a separately administered set of regulations. These are very similar to those provided under the FMLA, but contain subtle differences. So check with your employer about the specific details.

State employees. Congratulations! In the spring of 2003 the U.S. Supreme Court affirmed the right of the nearly 5 million state employees to coverage under FMLA, along with the right to sue for damages if they feel those rights have been violated.

Armed services. Members of the armed services are also entitled to family leave, but these programs are administered separately by the individual service branches. Parents in the military should check with their commanding officers about their eligibility for leave. Additional information can be found online at the Military Family Resource Center (http://mfrc.calib.com/index.htm).

Remember, every leave-taking situation is unique. To make the PDA and the FMLA work for you, you must be well-informed.

Teacher, Teacher . . .

Not all employment situations fit well within the provisions outlined by the FMLA. Teachers, for example, typically have a unique work-year calendar. All employees of private or public elementary and secondary schools are covered by a special set of provisions of the FMLA. The special rules do not apply to colleges and universities, trade schools, or preschools; employees of these institutions are covered by the normal provisions of FMLA (if they meet the basic employment standards defined by the law) and should check with their human resources department or union representatives for details.

＊ Coaches, driving instructors, special education, music, and art teachers, among other "special" teachers, are covered by the special rules. Classroom aides or assistants and "auxiliary personnel" such as psychologists, social workers, counselors, curriculum specialists, cafeteria workers, bus drivers, or maintenance workers are not. These employees are covered under the provisions of FMLA if they meet the regular criteria for coverage.

＊ Special rules apply to taking intermittent leave or leave on a reduced schedule. You cannot, for instance, work half-days or 3-day weeks as you ease back into full-time employment after giving birth or adopting a baby.

＊ A teacher beginning a leave near the end of the academic year may continue it at the beginning of the following academic year; summer vacation months that are not normally worked don't count against the leave. Any benefits normally provided during these vacation months must still be provided.

More information about how the FMLA applies to teachers can be found in the Department of Labor's full text of the law (Part F applies to teachers) at http://www.dol.gov/dol/allcfr/ESA/Title_29/Part_825/Subpart_F.htm.

Look up any details of the regulations you believe apply to your case and ask for help if you aren't sure how to untangle the red tape. If you do, chances are that by the time you announce your pregnancy to your employer and start working out the details of your leave, you'll know the relevant portions of these laws, and how they apply to you, inside and out.

SLIPPING BETWEEN THE CRACKS: WHAT IF I'M NOT COVERED BY FMLA?

The Family and Medical Leave Act was intended to revolutionize the way in which U.S. employers responded to the needs of employees trying to balance the demands of home and the workplace. For many women—and men—it has done just that, protecting their jobs while allowing them to take time off from work to spend with a newborn or a newly adopted baby (or cope with a seriously ill family member). Within the first 7 years after its implementation in 1993, more than 3.5 million employees took leave under FMLA, over a quarter of them to spend time with a new child.

But two groups of people have been unable to take advantage of the benefits offered under FMLA: employees who are covered under the act, but who simply cannot afford to take an unpaid leave of absence; and employees who are among the 38 percent of American workers whose employers are not bound by the provisions of FMLA, typically because they employ fewer than 50 individuals.

Let's look at the latter group first. About 60 percent of employers with between 25 and 49 employees offer FMLA coverage voluntarily, so don't automatically assume you aren't covered if you work for a small company. As of this writing, 17 states have family leave laws applying to employers of fewer than 50 workers; two states and Puerto Rico offer some coverage for all employees.

A far greater issue is that of unpaid leave. While 3.5 million people have taken family leave since its passage, an equal number of employees were eligible but weren't able to take leave, and 78 percent of them cited lack of income as the reason. Even more depressing is that nearly one out of 10 employees who took family leave with less than full income replacement reported they had to go on public assistance for all or part of their leave to make ends meet.

Consider the case of Peggy, 31, who works as a commercial insurance rater for a medium-sized company covered under FMLA. Her supervisor was happy about her pregnancy and encouraged her to take as much of her allotted 12 weeks off as she felt she needed. Peggy, whose husband Richard recently returned to school full time to get his MBA, would love to take a long leave; but as the family's only breadwinner, she simply couldn't take any time off without pay. She had 2 weeks of vacation time coming, and 2 additional weeks of accumulated sick days. Once these days were used up, Peggy was able to stay away from the office for only 1 unpaid week before the loss of income became a real problem. After only 5 weeks, Peggy had to return to work. "I didn't think it was supposed to be like this," Peggy says. "I was weepy and unhappy at work because I didn't feel ready to be away from Jake yet. I felt cheated, you know? I'll never get his early weeks back again."

FINDING THE MONEY

So what do you do? Well, the budget-planning sheet you completed in chapter 1 should come in handy now. Pull it out and take a careful look at where you might find some extra cash. Some possibilities:

Savings. Okay, it's not really income, but if you can, as soon as you know you are pregnant or as soon as you begin planning to become pregnant, start pinching those pennies. Cut corners in any large or small way you can, socking away "found money" (from gifts, overtime pay or extra work on the side, selling your great-grandmother's heirloom silver on E-Bay, giving up your monthly manicure or daily latte). You'll be amazed at how quickly it adds up.

Vacation, sick, and personal leave days. If you're planning to become pregnant or are already there, hoard these precious paid days off. Their accrued value can be taken as income during your leave—in fact, in most cases you must exhaust these when your leave begins.

Disability insurance. As of this writing, five states (California, Hawaii, New Jersey, New York, and Rhode Island) and Puerto Rico permit those on family leave to obtain partial wage replacement through the Temporary Disability Insurance (TDI) program. TDI is a state-administered program similar to the Unemployment Insurance program. It provides partial wage replacement to qualified employees who are temporarily unable to work because of an illness or injury. Ask your human resources representative whether some of your leave can be paid through this plan. Your health care provider will have to certify that you are unable to work for a certain number of weeks (typically 6 following a vaginal delivery; 12 after a cesarean) because of physical disability.

Unemployment insurance. Ask your employer whether you can collect income under your state-administered Unemployment Insurance (UI) program. A Department of Labor regulation passed in 2000 permits states to allow employees on family leave, though still considered to be employed, to receive partial wage employment through the UI system. So far, no state has yet taken advantage of the change in law and offered a plan to do this, but by the time you need it, your state may have become the first to do so.

With all of their shortcomings, the job-protection benefits available to new parents in the United States do offer a weak but vi-

Show Me the Money

The notion of a paid parental leave plan is popular with employees. Over 81 percent of U.S. employees polled recently expressed support for plans to make 12 weeks of leave available every year, with pay, for family and medical reasons. In reality, 34 percent of the women taking leave under FLMA receive no pay. Among those who receive some compensation during their family leave, wage replacement comes from a variety of sources, the least generous of which is an official, paid parental leave plan. Sources include:

Accumulated paid sick leave	61 percent
Accumulated paid vacation time	39 percent
Accumulated paid personal leave time	26 percent
Temporary Disability Income plans	18 percent
Other forms of compensation	11 percent
Paid parental leave plans offered by certain states or employers	8 percent

able safety net. For every parent unable to make use of FMLA, another is able to take a reasonable parental leave, often by cobbling together income from the sources listed above. Although there is little likelihood we'll see a nationally administered family leave plan with pay for many years, individual states are slowly but surely improving the paid leave situation by pressing for changes that will support growing families and offering wage replacement plans on a state-by-state basis.

KEYS TO KEEPING
THE BALANCE

The Pregnancy Discrimination Act, or PDA, protects you from being fired or otherwise discriminated against because you are pregnant.

The Family and Medical Leave Act (FMLA) guarantees job-protected family leaves of up to 12 weeks for employees who meet certain basic criteria at work to enable them to care for a new baby, an adopted baby, or a sick family member.

Unlike family leaves in many other nations, FMLA does not provide for paid leaves. Some states provide partial income replacement; other options include taking paid vacation and sick days and investigating income replacement through disability leave.

Family leave legislation is comprehensive in its scope and detailed in its application. A number of resources, including www.dol.gov and www.nationalpartnership.org, make it easy for you to determine exactly how the legislation applies to your situation.

If your company normally subsidizes your health insurance, it must continue to do so while you are on leave.

3

BREAKING THE NEWS

O ur husbands or partners are usually the first to hear. We can't wait to tell our mothers. Our best girlfriends can often tell from the look in our eyes even before we open our mouths. Whether it's your first baby or your fifth, there's nothing quite like the joy of letting people know you're pregnant. Why is it, then, that the thought of telling your boss makes you want to throw up even if you don't have morning sickness?

It shouldn't. After all, most of the time the telling goes well. Bosses are people, too, and they're often our colleagues and our friends as well as our employers. For instance, when Ellen, 25, a Gap store assistant manager, told her boss she was expecting her first child, tears welled up in his eyes. "You are going to be the *best* mother!" were his first words.

Of course, not everyone fares as well. Marianne, 33, a junior partner at a law firm where she has worked for 16 years since she was a high school student on an internship, felt as comfortable at work as she did in her home. Ed, a senior partner in the firm, had hired her to work during her college vacations, encouraged her to go to law school, and later made good on his promise to hire her full time. Marianne was almost as excited about telling Ed as she had been about telling her own parents.

His reaction, however, wasn't what she expected. "I thought you were serious about your career here, Marianne," were his first words. She was stunned. The company had a liberal and generous family leave policy that she herself had helped draft, and the pregnancies of several other women in the firm had been greeted with delight. "This is a really bad time for you to be out for months and months," Ed went on. The plan Marianne had so painstakingly drafted for her leave and return sat untouched on the chair as she fled the office in tears.

It took several more discussions once they'd both calmed down before they were able to get at the real issue. Ed's fatherly and protective attitude, rather than his respect for her professionalism, had come to the fore with her announcement, resulting in his disappointed reaction. Once the two talked about their complex relationship, he offered Marianne an even more generous leave package than she had planned to request, and made it clear that she was a valued colleague he was eager to see return.

PLANNING FOR SUCCESS

Of more than 4,000 women responding to an Internet survey conducted by BabyCenter.com, 83 percent said their employers were supportive when they told them about their pregnancies. But the odds of getting that support increase dramatically if you plan your announcement carefully. Regardless of what kind of work you do and what size company you work for, having a plan for breaking the news provides an element of control over how it will be received. And during this time of your life—when there is so little you *can* control—every little bit helps!

RESEARCH, RESEARCH, RESEARCH

Before you begin telling, you need to do some preliminary legwork to research your legal and situational options so you have a plan in hand when you share the happy news.

You did some of this work in chapter 1 when you answered questions to help you identify what you want in a leave as well as when you return. Go back to those notes. Did you envision as long a leave as you're entitled to? A short leave and a quick return to your job with leave days saved up like money in the bank? A custom-designed leave in which you and your husband or partner take intermittent leave so your baby has as much time as possible with each one of you?

Once you know what sort of leave you'd like, the next step is to put your plan into action. First, find out what, if anything, your employer offers in the way of job-protected leave, including any wage and salary replacement while you're on leave. If your company is large enough to have a personnel or a human resources department, you may have been given a copy of an employee handbook listing all personnel policies. If your company hasn't provided you with your own copy, make an appointment to see an office copy of this handbook. You are legally entitled to look at it without having to say why or to specify what policy or policies you're reviewing. It's a sort of don't-ask/don't-tell thing. Many companies also have this information on the company intranet, so you can look up family leave and other policies privately.

What if someone *does* ask what you're looking up? You can lie and say you were confused about vacation policy, finesse your answer by saying you just wanted to browse through a few sections pertaining to your job, tell her about your pregnancy (which you may not feel ready to do), or simply say you just want to do a little research on your own.

Make a copy of the policy or take notes as you read through it. Ask yourself these questions as you study the plan:

1. How much job-protected time off will my company give me? (Remember that companies covered under the provisions of FMLA

cannot give you shorter job-protected leaves than the FMLA or your state requires.)

2. Will I be paid all or part of my present salary or wage for some or all of this leave? For how long, and at what percentage?

3. Will I be required to use my accumulated vacation or sick time as a part of this leave?

4. If my husband and I work for the same company, are there special provisions covering when each of us may take time off?

5. Does my company's plan make provision for easing back into work at the end of my leave?

Some companies offer an even more generous family leave plan than that guaranteed by the government. For instance, IBM offers its employees 156 weeks of job-protected leave. It's unlikely your company will offer anything so generous, but it never hurts to check!

GATHERING INTELLIGENCE

Before you tell your boss the good news, there are other people you want to speak with—women at the office who have been in your shoes. Sit down somewhere private with a friend from the office (make sure she's someone who can keep a secret) and grill her on how it went when she announced *her* pregnancy. Was her supervisor receptive? Supportive? Caught off guard? Are there things your friend wishes she'd done differently?

For instance, Susan, a 35-year-old mother of 3-year-old twin girls, knew just what advice to give her friend, Audrey, about telling their mutual supervisor, Eleanor, about Audrey's pregnancy. "Eleanor desperately wanted children and couldn't have them," Susan told Audrey, "but she never talks about it at work. When I told her I was pregnant, she was pleased for me, but very emotional—she's the one who cried." Eleanor valued her personal and professional relationships with her staff, however, and Susan's pre-

When Your Boss Finds Out Before You're Ready to Tell

It's important that your employer doesn't hear about your pregnancy through the company grapevine before you're ready to tell. It this happens, your boss may be hurt or angry that you didn't come to her first. Most supervisors like to know what's going on with their staff. When your boss learns about your pregnancy from someone else, and then has to initiate the conversation with you—instead of the other way around—you lose that upper hand you've tried so hard to establish.

If your boss does pick up on the pregnancy scuttlebutt, speak with her as soon as possible. A good approach is something along the lines of "Oh, I can't believe I didn't get to tell you myself—I was so looking forward to sharing my news. At least we know we have an effective employee grapevine around here! I had planned to tell you as soon as I got my amnio results and was sure everything was going well." Emphasize that you were planning to make an appointment with her as soon as you had a rough plan for covering all your responsibilities during your leave.

diction that she would, ultimately, be pleased and supportive of Audrey, came true. "I was so glad to have been warned that this was a sensitive topic for Eleanor," Audrey says, "so I didn't go in there cheering like a kid at the circus."

THE THREE-PART PLAN
FOR ANNOUNCING YOUR PREGNANCY

There are three important elements to any plan for announcing your pregnancy:

* Whom to tell
* When to tell
* What to tell

Taking the Corporate Temperature

In addition to gathering information from coworkers about how your news might be received, take the measure of your corporate culture. Some informal clues about how working parents are viewed in your office or workplace are more telling than written policies.

　✳ Desks and cubicles. Are your colleagues' workspaces bright with kids' art thumbtacked to divider walls, and desktop photos of family members, or are personal or family-oriented items considered "unprofessional"?

　✳ Calendars. Is that company get-together in July a family affair? Does the CEO play Santa at a family Christmas brunch? Look at a friend's calendar—does her entry for a "doctor's appointment" really hide the date and time for her son's school play? Does the boss leave early on Wednesday nights to coach her daughter's soccer team? Does your supervisor ever move a meeting so she can make it to her son's music lesson?

　✳ Phone calls. Do a little eavesdropping. When parents call to check in with their day care providers, or to make sure their 11-year-olds have gotten home safely from school, do they phone from their desks, or do they make furtive, whispered calls in the bathroom from their cell phones?

　✳ Gender benders. Are men as likely as women to leave work for a parenting-related event? How many men take paternity leave, or walk over to the company's day care center to eat peanut butter sandwiches with their toddlers at noon?

Implementing each phase of the plan requires a certain amount of research and a little soul-searching. Knowing what you want in terms of not just your leave, but also the circumstances to which you return afterwards, will help guide you in developing your plan.

WHOM TO TELL

It's a good idea to get a sense—in your own head or actually written out as a plan, if you're a list-making kind of gal—of whom to tell, and when, and in what order. Besides your boss and your coworkers, you will want to inform, either formally or informally (through the grapevine or by letting them figure it out from your expanding waistline), any clients and customers with whom you work regularly. Each situation will differ according to a number of variables, including how often you work with a client, how important your personal relationship with them is, and whether you actually see them or are simply in phone or e-mail contact.

* First, tell any close friends you have at work. The initial disclosure should be the one that's going to be the most rewarding for you, and these are people you can trust to keep your secret to themselves until you give them the signal that it's time to let the cat out of the bag.

* Next, tell a few select people on the been-there/done-that list, other women who can share strategic advice about how to tell the big cheese.

* Tell the boss, after you do your legwork, before you begin to show, and before someone else can.

* Tell your co-workers, making it clear after the initial hoopla and congratulations that you're working out a plan for your leave that won't leave them in the lurch.

* Tell your clients and any outside vendors or consultants. This can wait a while, especially if you don't actually have face-to-face contact with them; but make sure you do this in time to assure them that their needs will be met and any necessary transitions will be handled smoothly.

* Tell customers on an as-needed basis. This may mean responding gamely to teasing and belly pats or simply letting a client with whom you speak on the phone once a week know that you're beginning your family leave in 2 weeks and that Marcus from your department will be handling their orders until you return.

A Class Act: Telling Your Students

When you tell your boss you're expecting, you probably don't have to worry that he's going to ask you where babies come from. If you're a teacher, though, you've got your own special class—no pun intended—of people to tell. "Telling my principal was easy, and she was delighted for me," says Rosa, 26, who teaches third grade. "But even though this is my first baby, I feel like I have 23 children already. I didn't want them to think I was abandoning them, and I was petrified someone would ask me exactly how I got pregnant!" In the end, no birds-and-bees lessons were requested. The children were thrilled, and immediately began making plans for a baby quilt they wanted to design and sew by themselves.

If you work with young children, there is an element of uncertainty in deciding when to tell. Child development experts note that kids under age 7 have an immature sense of time. The 5 or 6 months you may have left before your due date may seem like an eternity to them—or like no time at all. A good rule of thumb is to tell 1 month in advance of your due date (or planned departure date) for every year of the children's ages: if you're leaving your job in April, tell your preschoolers in January. Older kids (or their parents) may figure out what's up the first time you have to leave the class to throw up.

Rosa's concerns about what her children might have asked are also well founded. If you're an experienced teacher, it's likely nothing surprises you any-

WHEN TO TELL

Family leave law dictates that you must officially request your leave, stating a reason for your request, at least 30 days prior to the beginning of your leave (the law does make allowances for unexpectedly early deliveries or other crises). Of course, by your 8th month, someone just might have begun to suspect that trading in your form-fitting sheath dresses for baggy sweaters and elastic-panel slacks isn't just a funky new fashion statement on your part.

Sometimes the circumstances of your job compel you to share your news early. Carla, a 27-year-old supermarket cashier, wanted

more; but the questions that come out of the mouths of babes can throw even an expert. If your school has a social worker or psychologist available, ask them to help you formulate honest—but diplomatic—answers to potentially awkward questions. This is a good time to enlist the support of your kids' parents, making them partners in the education of their kids. The same day you tell your students, have a note ready for them to take home in their backpacks in which you break the good news to their parents. Give them a heads-up that at times like this, young students may begin to ask questions about where babies come from. Most parents will appreciate being able to supply these details themselves. If you teach in a middle or high school, just letting your students know your good news should be sufficient.

If you leave to have your baby in October, and come back in January, you may find yourself getting the cold shoulder from your youngest students upon your return. Just as infants and young children of working moms save up their frustrations and hurt feelings for their mothers at the end of the work day, your students may feel safe enough with you to risk letting you know they didn't like being left all alone (even if the substitute was terrific). Furthermore, now you don't belong just to them—you're somebody's *mom*. Take your cues from them and use a party or some other ritual to reconnect, and minimize the baby talk for a while unless they seem receptive to hearing about the newcomer in your life.

to remain at work as long as possible before beginning her leave, so she was in no hurry to let the manager of her department know she was pregnant. "I was only 14 weeks along, and not really showing—especially not under the smocks we wear at the store. But my feet finally made me talk. My job involves standing all day, and my tootsies and my back were already killing me!"

Carla finally gave in and alerted her supervisor to her condition. "She was pleasant enough about me being pregnant," Carla says, "but the real payoff was that she was really terrific about doing what she could to improve my working conditions. Now I have a tall chair at my register where I can sit if I need to, and she's giving me more frequent bathroom breaks—any pregnant woman can tell you how important that is! All in all, it worked out fine that I told earlier than I might have in a different line of work."

Joyce, a 34-year-old stock analyst, was comfortable in her desk job as her pregnancy proceeded, but laughs when she says there was little possibility of hiding the news that she was expecting. "The first time I had to run to the bathroom to throw up at work I was only 8 weeks along, but it happened that several people in the office had the stomach flu at the time, so no one paid much attention—they just sent me home to recover. Hah! Everyone else got over their flu, but I kept having to sprint to the bathroom, and I spent much of the day nibbling on saltines and sipping tea at my desk. One day I lost it over some pizza someone brought in for a party, and they all put two and two together. My coworkers figured it out before I could tell them!"

If your job involves conditions that are physically hazardous, or you work with toxic, heavy, or otherwise dangerous materials or machinery, you need to let someone know earlier than you might in a different job so accommodations can be made for your safety. When Jackie, a 26-year-old medical student, did an emergency medicine rotation that began early in the second trimester of her pregnancy, she had to be careful to avoid exposing herself to patients whose illnesses might harm her developing child. "I grabbed a chart one night while I was on duty and then hesitated when I saw the patient was a child who had cytomegalovirus, or CMV. This virus is known to pose significant risks to a developing fetus. As soon as I said, 'I can't take this patient—can someone else see him?' the staff all guessed why. They were all terrific about it, though, and helped me screen patients for any dangers after that."

When timing your announcement, also consider what else is

going on at work. Maybe the inventory project—or whatever the equivalent is for your workplace—didn't go so swimmingly after all. Maybe your boss's cat died last night. Maybe, like Susan, you have an employer or supervisor with unresolved fertility issues of her own, for whom hearing about staff pregnancies is sharply painful. Use your discretion about postponing your announcement. Conditions may not improve markedly, and you may need to tell for other reasons: so you can be up front about needing to make adjustments in your working conditions, or because you're tired of pretending your morning sickness is the Norwalk virus, or because you're just about to burst with excitement and can't wait to tell everyone else.

When to Tell Your Boss That You're Adopting

"My own boss explained it best," says Lenore, 37, a loan officer for a bank. "He told the other employees that it's just like it would be if I were pregnant, except that we don't know how long the pregnancy will last." There are no clear guidelines about when a prospective adoptive parent should tell her employer that she will need to take family leave, but she doesn't know exactly when the first day of her leave will start. Lenore told her boss as soon as she and her husband made it through their home study, and warned him that they could be bringing home the baby soon—or much later. With two adopted daughters of his own, he was delighted for them and allowed Lenore to take time off under FMLA to meet with adoption agency representatives and complete evaluations and paperwork.

Not all employers will be as understanding, of course. Stand firm, though, about your rights. If your company is covered under FMLA, families who are adopting a child receive all the benefits of FMLA. They also, unfortunately, are subject to the same shortcomings of the law: no mandated paid leave. They are free to seek income replacement through vacation and sick leave, however, or a more generous employer or state plan.

Barbara, 36, a benefits director for a large utility company, planned to tell her boss 2 weeks after her annual performance review. "It's not that I thought I'd get a bad review if my boss knew I was pregnant, or even that I thought I'd be taken less seriously if he knew. It just seemed to add one more variable to the mix, you know? I'd had a good year and accomplished a lot, and I didn't want to muddy the waters by introducing a new topic. I also had some plans for my department for the coming year, and I wanted to get a tentative go-ahead on these before they knew I'd be out for a couple of months. I ended up being pleased I'd waited. My performance review went well—so well, in fact, that I felt more confident when I went in to talk to my boss about my pregnancy and the leave I had planned. And because he was taking me quite seriously as an employee at that point, he was really supportive. In fact, he made a little joke, saying that was fine with him because now I was working for two!"

Is there a big project nearing completion in your office? Anxieties run high at times like this, and tempers get short. Anything that makes people think you might work with less enthusiasm, or be less available to your boss and your coworkers, just adds to an already stressful situation. So time your news to come *after* the project is done, the new client landed, or the grant application signed, sealed, and delivered. In fact, you may even get some extra Brownie points when you do tell. "My coworkers were amazed when I told them I was 14-weeks pregnant," says 27-year-old Ellen, a high school science teacher. "Our school was undergoing a rigorous accreditation review that required the teachers to put in long hours for weeks. There were so many nights when we worked until 10:00, then came back at 7:00 the next morning to teach. They were so impressed that I'd worked so hard without saying anything that people were making 'supermom' jokes!"

WHAT TO TELL

Today's the day. Your boss just got back from 2 weeks in Cancun and she's in a terrific mood. The big inventory project is over and came off without a hitch. You've laid the groundwork, you're well-informed about FMLA, your state's leave legislation, and what sort of leave your girlfriend got 6 months ago when her baby was born. You're even wearing your lucky earrings.

Most women find their bosses or supervisors are pretty laid back and reasonably supportive when they learn of an employee's pregnancy. "We want to keep good teachers," says one New England school superintendent. "And good teachers are good people, and good people usually want families. So many of our teachers are women in their childbearing years. I often even play a little game in my head and try to guess how many teachers in a given school will become pregnant during the school year. I'm usually pretty close, too. The bottom line for me is supporting these women and their families so they'll come back after they have their babies. We work with them to the extent our policy allows— and try to use the school year to be as flexible as we can—so they come back feeling comfortable and ready to be back in the classroom."

When you're ready to tell, remember:

Make an appointment. This is not the news to share on the fly when you pass your boss in the hall or happen to meet her at the copy machine. Arrange a time to sit down with her, one-on-one, when you can minimize distractions and interruptions. Choose your time—if you can—to coincide with a relatively calm time of day. Find a place where you can have some privacy, whether that's her office with the doors closed or the empty cafeteria.

Be happy. This sounds obvious, but some women are so anxious about telling their bosses, and concentrate so hard on behaving as professionally as possible about their announcement, that their bosses sometimes feel compelled to ask, "Are you pleased?" or "This is great news! Um, isn't it?"

Never apologize. Even if you're aware that you will be leaving your position in the middle of the spring rush, or the fall sales season, don't say you're sorry. You haven't done anything wrong, you're just having a baby!

Show your smart side. Matter-of-factly let it be known that you are aware of your rights. You might casually say: "Now, I've spoken with Molly in Human Resources several times, and I'm so pleased that our company leave plan goes a bit beyond what's offered under FMLA."

Give your boss a role. Even if you have the plan all worked out, it doesn't hurt to find a way for your boss to have some input. You could say: "Because Allied Widget company offers as much as 24 weeks of leave, I'd like to take 18 full weeks off—staying in touch with the office, of course—and use the remaining 6 weeks to ease back in by working part time. How do you think this will work for our department? I could make it 16 full weeks and 8 half, if that works better for you." Be careful, though; don't offer items as options that you feel you *must* have, and to which you know you're legally entitled.

Have a written plan. Write up the details of how you envision your leave, but don't cast anything in stone. Also, add a few phrases that allow you to make changes as needed (such as "Assuming that my pregnancy continues to go well . . ." and "We can make adjustments to this plan as necessary should circumstances change"). For a sample letter, see "Put It in Writing" on page 64. Later in this book, we'll talk about how to write a comprehensive plan to cover issues that might arise during your absence.

Now I Know More than My Boss Does!

You may well end up knowing more about family leave policies than your boss does. A Congressional study of how well family leave legislation is working found, among other things, that accurate information about the law is not always easy to come by in the workplace. In fact, only about one out of four women surveyed during this study had heard about FMLA from their employer. They were far more likely to have gotten their information from television, family members, or their unions.

It's true that it may not really be your supervisor's job to stay up to date on the intricacies of federal employment law. This is, after all, why you have a human resources department. And it's why you're doing so much of the homework yourself. But a boss who greets the news of your pregnancy by saying "Hey, that's terrific! So you gonna take 5 or 6 weeks off?" may not be delighted to hear that you know you're entitled—if your company is covered under FMLA—to at least 12 weeks of leave. Such a boss may be even less thrilled that you are more in the know than he is. So here are your options:

✳ Say sweetly but firmly, "In fact, I am planning to take the full 12 weeks offered by federal law. Here's the plan I've drawn up."

✳ Laugh and say, "Well, under my present circumstances, I've found the FMLA fascinating reading. I'd be glad to share with you what I've learned."

✳ Politely offer to update him. If your boss is really uncertain about what the law provides, tell him you'll be happy to bring him a copy of it. Remember, you're not asking for his approval; but anything you can do to make him better informed and help him to understand the law will benefit both you and other moms-to-be who follow in your footsteps.

✳ Under no circumstances shake your head girlishly and say, "Oh, okay, I guess 6 weeks will be enough."

FMLA is there, it's the law, and it's yours. Use it.

Show off your research. Let your boss know that you understand the impact your temporary absence may have. For instance, when Juliet, a 28-year-old manager of a publishing firm's art department, told her supervisor that she'd be taking off, she quickly set her boss's mind at ease about going AWOL during a very busy time.

"This does mean I'll be out during the period when we usually start assembling the spring catalog," Juliet told her boss, "so I've put together some plans to make sure there won't be any gaps in coverage or any delays in getting the layout done." She also outlined how she would maintain communication with her staff, supervisor,

Put It in Writing

After you inform your boss of your plan to take family leave, you'll still want to put it in writing so that you both have a written record for your files. Since there's no way to know for certain when your leave will need to start, try to give yourself some leeway. Here's a sample letter to get you started.

February 23, 2004
Dear Alice,

As you and I discussed last week in your office, I am expecting a baby in early July and plan to begin my Family and Medical Leave shortly before I'm due to deliver. Assuming that all goes according to plan, my last day will be on or around June 30. I expect to return to work on a part-time basis in early September, and be back at my job full time by October.

Thanks again for your support and good wishes. I'll be keeping you posted about my current projects and how they might best be handled during my leave.

Sincerely,
Angela Jones

and, as necessary, outside vendors, during her leave. Juliet's boss was impressed and pleased that her commitment to the project would not fall by the wayside during her absence.

Pull a Schwarzenegger. Reassure your supervisor with an "I'll be back." This is not the time to raise the possibility that you might not return to your job following the baby's birth. Even if you are reasonably sure that you want to be a stay-at-home mom, or shift to part-time or a different line of work, there will be plenty of time later to burn bridges. In chapter 10, we'll talk about what happens if you decide not to return after your leave. For now, let your boss and your colleagues assume you will be returning by sharing with them your plan for reentry. Remember how unpredictable pregnancy can be—your financial situation may change, your job may change—hey, you might not *like* being a stay-at-home mom. Leave your options open.

INTERVIEWING WHILE YOU'RE PREGNANT

It's one thing to be in the middle of a cushy (or not so cushy) job knowing that, even if your employer isn't thrilled that you're going to be on leave soon, you're at least still protected against pregnancy-based discrimination. It's quite another to find yourself job hunting for two.

If you lose your job while you're pregnant (I'm going to assume it wasn't *because* you're pregnant), and you aren't showing yet, or if you become pregnant during the job hunt, what do you do? Do you have to tell an interviewer or prospective employer that you're expecting? What if the interviewer brings up the topic of pregnancy or asks about your future plans to balance work and parenting? Just because it's illegal for a prospective employer to ask about pregnancy, it doesn't mean much if they do anyway. After all, jumping up and yelling, "You aren't allowed to ask me that!" ranks pretty low on the list of successful job-hunting techniques.

One approach is to be proactive and bring up the subject yourself, employing some of the same tactics you might use if you were presenting a plan for your family leave in an existing job. Don't make the impending baby your opener, but after you've established some rapport with your interviewer you might say, "I'd like to share with you that I'm expecting. I have some ideas about how I'd handle my pregnancy and family leave on this job." Obviously, you don't know the other staff members, but you can stress that one of your first priorities will be to engage your staff and work with your colleagues to establish a plan to ensure that your department's obligations are fulfilled.

If you would rather not disclose your pregnancy to a potential employer at this stage, it is entirely within your rights not to do so. Be aware that if you choose this route, though, you will need to be especially discreet about whom you do tell. It's easy enough not to mention your pregnancy in your interviews, but someone on your list of references could spill the beans. And while you could tell any of your references who do know that you hope they will not volunteer that you're pregnant, it's bad business karma—not to mention just plain unethical—to ask them to tell outright lies on your behalf.

Consider the case of Corona, who was a 29-year-old graduate student in the English department of a small midwestern college when she found out she was pregnant. It was a month before a major academic conference at which she planned to do some serious job hunting in what she knew was an already crowded field. "I felt a little dishonest, but I just didn't want anyone to know I was pregnant until I had a job nailed down. My field is so competitive that any element that might make a potential employer think I'd be high maintenance had to be kept under wraps. My boyfriend and I didn't even tell any of our closest friends until after I'd done all my interviewing at the conference and gotten a tentative offer." Corona landed an assistant professorship at a small southern university. "They were a little flustered when I accepted the job and added 'by the way, I'm expecting a baby in July,'" she said. "But at least I was able to be on the job when classes started in September. Once they asked, 'Were you pregnant when we met you at the MLA conference?' and I just laughed and said 'Not very!'"

The main advantage of concealing your pregnancy during the hiring period, as Corona did, is that it will most likely make it easier to be hired. Though it is virtually impossible to prove that you were discriminated against because of your pregnancy, it does happen.

There are, however, some disadvantages that can arise from not disclosing your pregnancy before you're hired:

* The fact that you will have been on the new employer's payroll for a relatively brief period before your baby is born means that you will not be eligible to take job-protected leave under the provisions of FMLA. Unless your employer or your state has a more generous family leave policy than that offered under the federal law, you will be at the mercy of the good graces of your new boss when it comes to arranging leave and making plans to return to work.

* Your new boss may be resentful that you weren't straight with her. Anna, 26, interviewed for an entry-level broker's position with a small financial services firm. Tall but slightly built, Anna had been able to disguise her 6-month pregnancy by dressing carefully. "I figured if they noticed, I'd tell them that yes, I was pregnant, but if they

didn't notice or mention it, I wasn't going to," she says. "They didn't notice, I got the job, and I waited 2 weeks before breaking the news. Susan, my new boss, admitted that she might well have done the same thing in my shoes, but it was also clear that she was put out and that I'd lost some credibility in her eyes."

✳ You may feel that you have to curtail your leave to keep your job or your standing in the new company. Anna felt pressured to return to work after only 8 weeks of leave. "On top of that, I worked my butt off when I got back and only really felt forgiven after another 6 months of being a really conscientious, high-producing employee."

Susan, who hired Anna, confirms that Anna read her reaction correctly. "She was just what we wanted in an employee, and though I fully understand why she made the decision not to tell, it did leave us in the lurch when she took leave less than 3 months after starting. It was tough for me as her boss, and for coworkers who had to pick up slack for her, that as soon as she was fully trained, she was gone for 2 months. I confess I was a little ticked off at her for a long time afterwards."

Corona's department head had similar concerns. "Yes, technically she was ready to be in the classroom when the fall semester began, but she missed a lot in terms of getting to know the other members of the department. The faculty could have been a lot of help to her as she began her first full-time teaching position; and between being on leave and being understandably focused on her new baby, she felt like a stranger to us for most of the first year."

Think about issues like these as you plan ahead. Remember, your goal isn't simply to be hired, but to remain in this job as long as it is a fulfilling and profitable one for you. It is in your best interest to be honest about your condition as soon as you feel comfortable doing so, and to plan ahead to cushion the impact of your impending leave to the extent that you can.

THE NEWS IS OUT!

Once you've told your supervisor and a few coworkers, the news will spread quickly throughout the office. Hopefully, your boss's re- action was positive and your coworkers are also pleased for you. Your chances of this scenario coming true are greatly improved if you've handled the announcement as I've outlined in this chapter: reassuring them you aren't leaving first thing in the morning, thinking ahead to how your job will get done while you're gone, preparing for your return. Later in the book, I'll talk more about how to deal with your coworkers throughout your pregnancy.

For now, enjoy being the "It" girl as the news gets around. Sud- denly you're the flavor of the week. Everyone's buzzing about your news, dropping by your desk to hear how you're feeling, when you're due, and to tease you about how much weight you've gained, even if you've been so nauseous that you've actually *lost* weight. Pregnant women are like magnets—people just seem drawn to them, unable to resist being part of the excitement. When you think about it, it makes sense. There you are, in the middle of the office or the shop or the store, and while everyone around you is composing let- ters or assembling widgets, you're simultaneously doing something else: You're making a new person.

KEYS TO KEEPING THE BALANCE

X Make sure you have your ducks in a row before telling anyone about your pregnancy—know your rights under FMLA and find out what your company's leave policies are.

X Tell a few trusted friends at the office who have been there themselves and see what advice they have to offer. Then tell your boss or supervisor, and only then share the news with the rest of the staff.

X Don't make it appear as though you're dictating your company's leave policy to your boss; leave some room for negotiation on her behalf and yours. Working together will make your leave-planning go more smoothly.

X If you're interviewing for a job while pregnant, you are not legally obligated to tell your potential employer about your pregnancy. You may, however, choose to be proactive and bring up the topic yourself. If you choose to wait until after you're hired, tell your supervisor as soon as you feel comfortable doing so, and plan ahead to cushion the impact of your impending leave to the extent that you can.

X Don't panic—remember that most of these announcements go over very well.

4

A FIELD GUIDE
TO OFFICE FAUX PAS—
THEIRS AND YOURS

N ot everyone in your workplace will greet the news of your pregnancy matter-of-factly, either initially or in the long run. Even good friends at your job who are delighted for you may have some unexpected, disconcerting, or hurtful reactions. The trick is to try to manage people's reactions and their treatment of you. The best way to control the situation, as with any management issue, is to be proactive. Take the right steps ahead of time to keep things running on an even keel, even before you announce that a baby is coming.

First, as we discussed in chapter 3, it's important that you understand your corporate culture. Even if your "corporation" is a small preschool or a family-run restaurant, you need to get a handle on how your coworkers feel about babies in general, and about you having one. Babies—even before they make their arrival—are powerful little critters who evoke strong (and sometimes strange) reactions in those around them. Be prepared for the fact that your announcement and ongoing pregnancy will inspire different reactions depending on your workplace; a laid-back company will react one way, a company that thrives on deadlines and crises, another.

If, right about now, you're thinking that your pregnancy is *your* business, think again. There's no escaping the fact that your pregnancy *will* affect other people in the workplace. No matter how dedicated, organized, and committed you are to your job, eventually something related to your pregnancy will have an impact—or a perceived impact—on your work. Take the case of Sarah, 36, a trial attorney in a high-powered law firm. She worked hard throughout her pregnancy, taking great pains not to let it affect her on-the-job performance. She got to work on time, took care not to leave early, and was even able to arrange most of her prenatal care visits for lunch hours and holidays. She was startled, therefore, when just before a Monday staff meeting during her 7th month, after a coworker asked how she was feeling, the senior partner said acidly, "Could we save the baby talk for after the meeting, ladies? It seems like all we ever do around here is talk about Sarah's baby!"

Sarah was floored, but managed to keep her composure. Knowing that the senior partner was the sort of guy who likes to keep the focus on himself and control the agenda didn't make his remark any less frustrating. But by taking a moment to think about his priorities, Sarah was able to let the comment pass without taking it too personally.

Likewise, the better you're able to anticipate how your coworkers will react to your pregnancy, the better you'll be able to address their concerns or respond to any resentment. No matter what, though, don't apologize for your pregnancy or how it affects your day-to-day functioning. Pregnancy isn't a crime (even if your boss or the gal in the next cubicle may sometimes act as if it is), and it isn't something you arranged just to spite the folks at work.

Be as professional as you were before the pregnancy, or maybe even a little more. And even though your sweatpants may look particularly inviting right now, be careful to follow the dress code in your office. If you work in a conservative environment, you'll find numerous tips on dressing professionally for two in chapter 7. If you work in a jeans-and-sweaters auto parts store, or wait tables in a uniform, do what you can to minimize the difference between what you used to wear before your stomach began expanding, and what you wear now. How you present yourself—both in the clothes you wear and the attitude you take—will go a long way in how your coworkers treat you and your pregnancy.

CONSIDER THEIR PERSPECTIVE

One of the best ways to manage a coworker's thoughtlessness or nosiness is to take a deep breath and imagine where the motivation for such statements comes from. Most of the time, your coworkers' motivations will boil down to one (or more) of the following:

Awe. Let's face it, having a baby is about the most astounding thing a woman can do. The fact that we can grow a living, breathing, brand-new human being right in our own personal incubator and still manage to drive cars, perform surgery, turn out wedding cakes, balance spreadsheets, play piano, teach calculus, or whatever it is our particular job requires is nothing short of incredible. People tend to react to moms-to-be in much the same way that they'd react if they ran into a minor movie star coming out of Starbucks: with tongue-tied, stammering, fan-crazed idiocy.

Ignorance. Within weeks of your conception—if not earlier— you're already well on your way to becoming a pregnancy expert. If "pregnancy" were a category on *Jeopardy*, you'd be going home with pockets full of green; if it were on the final exam, you'd be *summa cum laude*. Take it for granted that most of your coworkers haven't boned up recently on human lactation, endocrinology, fer-

73

tility, or the Tao of T. Berry Brazelton. Cut 'em a little slack as they pepper you with infantile questions, and gently educate them along the way.

Envy. Freud must have been absent the day they discussed pregnancy envy, but every woman who's pregnant can tell you that it rears its ugly head far too often and usually unexpectedly. This one's a double-whammy, because not only may people be jealous of all the attention you're getting, but also they may be jealous of your ability to become pregnant, especially if they have fertility problems of their own. (Never mind that you may have had a difficult time getting pregnant.)

Superiority. Did you take fertility drugs? Must be something wrong with you (or—nudge, nudge, wink, wink—him). Not planning to breastfeed? Hrmph—some mother *you're* going to be. Face it—there's not one of us without our own personal areas of insecurity. Seeing someone pull off any difficult task—and balancing work and pregnancy is wa-a-a-y far up on the list of life's difficult tasks—pushes some people's buttons in a weird way. They may react by subtly (or not so subtly) letting you know that they know better/do better/plan better. It's incredibly annoying, but this kind of behavior is so much a fact of life that you're better off ignoring it instead of stewing over it.

Anger. Add up all of the above, and what you might get hit with is anger. Not because your coworker is really mad at *you*—but because you're getting all the raves right now, because something exciting is happening to you and not to them, because they hate this stinking, lousy job already and it's only going to get worse when you go on leave and everyone else's workload doubles overnight.

Not all motives for the inappropriate comments people make to pregnant women are misguided. For women who are just a little bit behind you on the mommy ladder, you may be a shining

Things We'd Love to Hear About Our Pregnancies

* Congratulations!
* You look fabulous—pregnancy really suits you.
* Let me know if there's anything I can do for you.
* I have some wonderful clothes from my last pregnancy that I think would fit you. You're welcome to borrow them.
* You look tired—if you want to close your door and catch 40 winks, I'll handle your calls.

example, a role model, and a potential mentor. Just observing how you handle hurdles such as morning sickness, make family leave plans, or get through the revolving doors in your office building's lobby is like taking a crash course in on-the-job pregnancy. They may genuinely wonder what the current medical thinking is on pregnancy weight gain, or whether it's safe for you (and later, them) to fly to the conference in Cleveland in your 6th month, or how one manages to look professional while throwing up twice a day.

In addition, certain categories of pregnancy and parenting issues are emotional touchstones for other parents or parents-to-be. People like to share their stress; they like some reassurance that they aren't bad parents. If you're planning to come back to work only 8 weeks after your baby is born, maybe that will help to settle some of the ambivalence a coworker feels when she took a shorter leave than the one offered to her. Maybe if you can balance pregnancy—and later, motherhood—and the job you love, she can, too.

So try to distinguish between those coworkers who are simply being nosy or thoughtless and those seeking real information that they might apply to their own situations. And keep in mind, too, that some people simply aren't very good at office small talk and will jump at the opportunity for conversation that your newly announced pregnancy affords.

THE RIGHT COMEBACK

No matter how skillfully you announce your pregnancy, and how low-key you are about this miracle you're producing, there will still be people at work who are simply unable to take things in stride and go on quietly writing annual reports or cranking out widgets or publishing magazines, or whatever it is they do when they could be managing your life, medical care, and family dynamics instead. So here's a field guide to some of the most difficult denizens of Pregnancyville and how to handle them safely.

The Pregnancy Police. You sit down at your desk with a steaming cup of organically grown, water-decaffeinated, midwife-approved tea, and the Pregnancy Police kick into action: "Should you be drinking that? That could really hurt your baby, you know!" Heaven forbid you should take a sip of champagne at your own baby shower, or let it slip that you're going to the gym to do a couple of miles on the treadmill. If you do, some well-intentioned but misguided soul is certain to give you the third-degree about whether you should do that in your delicate condition.

Solution: Gently thank the caffeine cops and their ilk for their concern, firmly adding that your doctor has already signed off on all of your activities.

Smokers' Delight. You've taken to bringing your lunch every day and enjoying it on a little bench on the sunny side of your office building. Because your office is smoke-free, the smokers in the office also gravitate to this spot with their lunches. You don't want to be rude, so you suffer in silence as the blue-gray haze thickens around you.

Solution: It sounds like you've just discovered the prime lunch time real estate your nicotine-addicted friends staked out some time ago. If you were there first, you can certainly say, "I'm so sorry, but the smoke from your cigarettes is making me feel nauseous—and it's so bad for the baby." They may apologize and stub out their cigarettes, or they may not, suggesting, instead, that you lunch elsewhere. You get upset when people police your health habits, so it isn't right for you to try to control theirs. Within the office, however, you are well within your rights (if, indeed, your office is one of the last remaining smokers' havens in the country) to raise awareness of the dangers of secondhand smoke for pregnant women and their babies.

Diet Divas. No matter how many times you've spoken with your health care provider about your weight gain and been assured you're doing fine, someone at your workplace is bound to know better. Have a chef salad in the cafeteria and the Diet Divas will urge you to throw caution to the wind and have the chocolate cake. "After all, you're eating for two now!" Have the chocolate cake, though, and the next Diet Diva who walks by will wink knowingly and ask, "Eating again, eh?"

Solution: Stick to the healthy diet your health professional recommended. Then wink back as you pick up the next forkful and say quite happily: "Just what the doctor ordered!"

The Infertility Goddess. Your best friend at the office has spent 3 years and a tremendous sum of money on fertility treatments that, so far, haven't worked. Although she's happy for you, you can't help but notice the stricken look on her face every time your pregnancy is mentioned. Should you stop talking about your pregnancy?

Solution: You don't need to censor every mention of pregnancy in your conversations, but you may want to downplay your glee and be careful not to say anything insensitive ("I got pregnant the first month we started trying. It was so *easy!*"). At the same time, don't be glib about her prognosis. Saying "I know you'll be pregnant soon, too," is not very helpful. You don't know this at all. While you can't be in charge of relieving her grief, you can at least not exacerbate it. If you're close enough, you might talk with her about her feelings and ask what you can do to help or at least not make things any harder for her. Try saying, "I know this must be very hard for you, all the attention I've gotten here at the office since I announced my pregnancy. Is there anything I can do to make it easier for you?" If she demurs, let it go, but if she wants to talk, let her. She probably isn't so much resentful of you as she is simply sad for herself.

Adoption Analyzers. As insensitive as some of the comments made to pregnant women can be, people who are waiting to adopt may hear things that are simply appalling: "I heard that you're adopting—couldn't you have a real baby?" or "At least you won't need a maternity leave."

Solution: Waiting to adopt a child is a little different from being pregnant at work. You're about to become a mother just like your round-bellied coworker, but chances are you don't garner nearly the same attention and support she does. If you're waiting to adopt, you may not know how long it will be before your child arrives, how much notice you will have, or whether the adoption will come through at all.

Education is one of the best routes here. Simply talk with your coworkers about some of the uncertainties that could affect your work schedule ("I may not have much notice when the baby is ready for us to bring home, so I'm working to keep my projects up to date and my agenda organized. I've asked Jeff to work with me on these, so if I have to leave suddenly, he'll be up to speed on what's happening in my department."). Make it clear, though, that you consider yourself to be expecting, even if your baby may come by airplane. Chances are your excitement and sense of anticipation will transmit themselves to your colleagues and they'll be supportive and anxious right along with you.

The Horror King (or Queen). Closely related to the Pregnancy Police, but somewhat less well-intentioned, the horror monarch is the Wes Cravens of the pregnancy world. His or her job is to share with you every awful pregnancy, labor, and delivery story known. Did you hear about the pregnant woman over in accounting who tried to finish a report after her water broke and ended up giving birth in the company elevator? Or about poor Diane in the mailroom who was on her feet too long during the third trimester and gave birth to a perfect little baby the size of a lima bean? Hang around this one too long and you'll hear both of these—and plenty more like them.

Solution: Be firm about canning this horror script. "I'm sure there's research showing that stories like these are very harmful to pregnant women. You'll understand, then, that I don't want to hear any more of them." If you run into a repeat performance, leave the room.

The Joker. This is the guy who corners you in the coffee room and loudly announces: "Yeah, breast feeding's a wonderful thing, isn't it? The milk is always ready, it's up high where the cat can't get it, and it comes in such cute packages!" He's got a million of 'em, and he's saving them all for your weekly staff meeting.

Solution: Look him in the eye and say: "Don't quit your day job, Al. Next item on the agenda?"

The Child Protection Agent. This one has all the advice you never want to receive about what to do after the baby comes. "I could never put my child in someone else's hands—did you see that thing in the paper about the baby who died when the day care lady left him in the hot car?"

Solution: If a slow, steady stare doesn't make this one think twice about opening her mouth to you ever again, sweetly say, "That *was* terrible, wasn't it?" and go on about your work.

The Mommy Devaluer. This one is known for saying things like, "Once that baby comes, he's all you'll ever think about. You won't ever want to come back to work, but be sure and visit us working stiffs sometimes."

Solution: Statements like these can usually be translated: "Once you have that baby, we're afraid you won't care about us any more and we'll be left to do all your work." So don't let coworkers taunt you into revealing the details of your post-leave plans before you're ready. Remind your coworkers that you're working out a plan with your supervisor to make sure everything is covered. Speak often about events in the post-delivery future: "I hope I can count on you to work with me on plans for the annual conference again."

The Rugrat Resenter. This is the coworker who gets mad at you before you're midway through your second trimester because he's sure you're going to leave a pile of work undone that he'll have to do, just as he's sure he'll have to cover for you as you flit about taking the new arrival for check-ups, express breast milk, and eat bon bons.

Solution: No amount of pre-baby planning will make this guy happy, so don't even try. Sure, you can make certain he's aware of your plans for coverage, but the best response is just to sit back and do your work. It also helps if, whenever possible, you can wave goodbye to him as he passes you on his way home at 4:30, calling out, "Wow, is it 5 o'clock already?"

The Octopus. What is it about a pregnant woman's belly that makes everyone in the world want to touch it? The men—and the women—in your office have suddenly gotten worse than 10th graders on their second date: all hands.

Solution: You've got to admit that the growing globe you're carrying is so irresistible it practically glows. No wonder everyone wants to touch you, pat you, hug you. Sure, it's inappropriate to grab someone without permission, and you can tell them to keep their grubby paws to themselves, but this is a case in which a little tolerance and humor might work better. Try saying to the next person who reaches for you: "Be careful! This one bites."

Copyroom Casanova. The first time he says it, standing casually beside you waiting for a turn at the copy machine, you are mildly flattered. "You know, pregnant women look really sexy. I hope your husband appreciates you." The next time it's not so welcome, and the time after that is downright creepy.

Solution: Speak up. Of course pregnant women are sexy, but sexual harassment is real—and against the law. Tell Casanova that his comments make you uncomfortable and you want them to end.

And the Winner Is . . .

A 2003 ePregnancy magazine poll revealed that the most annoying behavior on the part of strangers toward a pregnant woman was their insistence on delivering unsolicited advice. Survey participants also cited belly touching, lack of courtesy, making inappropriate comments, and pointing or staring.

Document all such encounters, and if they persist, report them to your supervisor.

Intimate Invaders. There are obnoxious things to ask a pregnant woman, and then there are things that go so far beyond rudeness that you may actually gasp. Things like: "So, you must be having some prenatal testing. What do you think you'll do if the tests show that there's a problem?" "Triplets? Whadja do—overdose on fertility drugs?" "Your breasts are kind of small for a pregnant woman's— think you'll really be able to breastfeed?"

Solution: Sometimes you just have to be blunt. Give them the benefit of your (slim) doubt, but be firm: "I'm sure you don't mean to be offensive, but this isn't really any of your business."

The God Squad. These cheerfully righteous individuals take it upon themselves to not only worry about your morning sickness and swollen ankles, but also about your immortal soul. Their input may range from mild (if nosy) curiosity ("So, are you having the baby christened at your church?") to a little over the line ("I've brought you this wonderful book of prayers for mothers-to-be") to over-the-top meddling (expressing their concerns that your mixed-religion marriage will be bad for the baby).

Solution: Regardless of whether you share their religious beliefs, it is not appropriate for said beliefs to be thrust upon you, especially on the job. Again, a firm hand is essential: "I appreciate your concern, but these are personal issues I'd rather not discuss with you."

WATCH YOUR MANNERS

Even more obnoxious than the Pregnancy Police is a Pregnancy Princess, someone who neglects to mind her own manners and ends up offending her coworkers with her lack of consideration.

When There's Bad News

Approximately 20 percent of all pregnancies end in miscarriage, most of them during the first trimester or early in the second trimester. If you're working while you're pregnant and you lose the baby or make the difficult decision to terminate the pregnancy, you will be faced with one of two situations: maybe you've already told your boss and coworkers you're pregnant, received their congratulations and attention, and now have to tell them things have changed; or you may have to explain that you're no longer expecting even before you told them you were pregnant.

If the latter applies to you, you also have the option of not mentioning the miscarriage at all. Much about how you handle this situation depends on the atmosphere at your workplace, the relationships you have with the people there, and how you feel physically and emotionally following the miscarriage. In either case, talking about your miscarriage at work may bring some unintentionally hurtful, shortsighted, or just plain ignorant comments from coworkers:

> "Hey, that's awful! I guess it just wasn't meant to be."
>
> "Yeah, happened to me twice. You've just gotta forget about it and move on."
>
> "So, what happened exactly?"
>
> "Do you think it was because you're working so many hours?"

It may also bring you the support you need, as it did for Marianne, an account executive for a soft-drink bottler. "My husband and I received a gift certificate for dinner for two at our favorite restaurant from my boss, with a card that read simply, 'I'm sorry. Bob,'" she recalled. "And when I returned to work after a couple of days off, he urged me to take it easy and take care of myself, and to let him know if I wanted more time off. The people at work sort of modeled their approach on his, and everyone was very sympathetic in a low-key way, very respectful of my privacy."

If your boss or coworkers are well-meaning but not sensitive, you may have to say, gently but firmly, "Thank you for thinking of me—I appreciate everyone's sympathy, and I just want to get back to work now. I'm sure you'll understand."

It's important, after all, to hold up your end of the stick after the stick turns blue. Here are some common faux pas you'll want to avoid:

Global warming. It's fine to say, "Wow, is it hot in here, or is it just me?" as your internal thermometer goes into overdrive. It's rude to insist that the office thermostat continually be adjusted to accommodate your hormone-driven heater. If you're soaking up the air conditioning while everyone else is pulling on sweaters and ski caps, you may need to be a bit less self-centered. Turn the thermostat back up, dress more lightly, and buy yourself a small fan.

Whine and cheese. "You guys *know* I can't eat/drink this right now! Didn't anyone think to bring any ginger ale to this cocktail reception?" Plan ahead and bring your own provisions or just make do, but don't expect others to wait on you hand and foot.

Too-proud mama. The film from your latest ultrasound is burning a hole in your purse and you can't wait to show everyone at the staff meeting the irrefutable evidence that your baby is a boy.

Six Ways to Say "None of your Business"

* That's something my husband/partner/doctor/midwife and I have already worked out.
* Thank you for your concern.
* I'd rather not talk about it.
* My, that's awfully personal.
* What a question!
* That's none of your business.

But for some people, viewing any ultrasound printouts except their own is right up there with watching someone get her tongue pierced. Even people who profess to be fascinated are likely to point to Junior's photogenic little head and cry, "Look at the tiny heart!" Save the pics for your partner, parents, and best girlfriends and assure your coworkers that your ultrasound shows everything is going well.

The incredible shrinking work ethic. "I don't think my doctor would like me to lift that." "Stress is very bad for babies, you know—I'm going home early to rest." "Sorry I'm late (again). I'll make it up to you by coming in early tomorrow. I mean it this time." Sure, pregnancy can make you tired or nauseous, and there are things you should not do while you're expecting. But monitor yourself to make sure you aren't saying "no" (or "me, me, me") too often. Focus on getting the job done and making sure your coworkers know that work is still your top priority.

No matter how upset you may get on a day when everyone seems to violate your personal space, question your motives, your maturity, and your responsibility, no matter how often you are poked, prodded, patted, and patronized, it is not a good idea to give free rein to your hormones and have a temper tantrum.

Because then you would have to say, crescendoing from a frustrated squeak to a dull roar: "What is the matter with you people?! Have you never seen a pregnant woman at work in all your born days? Have you never read Dr. Spock or *What to Expect When You're Expecting* or heard of obstetric care or seen a woman nurse a baby? I am pregnant, not helpless, not stupid, not lazy—PREGNANT—hear me roar!"

No, you would never say that. At least, not out loud.

KEYS TO KEEPING THE BALANCE

Babies and pregnancies evoke powerful reactions. Some people are loving and supportive, but others can be offensive, angry, envious, harassing, or just plain rude.

Be aware that your behavior affects others. Hold up your end of the stick at work, and don't hog all of the attention or be a prima donna. Maintaining a professional manner will set the standard for how people treat you and your pregnancy.

Try to understand the point of view or the motivation of people saying offensive or stupid things. They may mean well and don't mean to upset you.

Be firm with people who are genuinely offensive or whose actions constitute harassment.

Although a sarcastic response may be on the tip of your tongue, humor mixed with information is usually a more effective approach in the long run.

PREGNANCY SYMPTOMS
ON THE JOB

For all the excitement, wonder, and joy they bring, pregnancies can also be downright awful. "I had every pregnancy symptom known to womankind," says Tyra, 34, a sales representative for a pharmaceutical company. "I ached everywhere, had to pee every 5 minutes, developed gestational diabetes, had wicked heartburn and backaches—and don't even get me started about the morning sickness! More like all-day sickness. Making my sales rounds was a nightmare, and of course everyone guessed I was pregnant before I would have told them because I was always running to throw up."

Other women, however, seem to sail through their 9 months without a hitch. Jenny, 29, a veterinarian, says she never felt better than during her first pregnancy. "I was pretty tired during the first trimester, but by the time I was 4 months along, I had this incredible energy and never really had any symptoms that bothered me. My husband and I are trying now for a second child, and I'm actually looking forward not just to having another baby, but to the pregnancy itself."

Which pregnancy is normal? Both. And neither. No two pregnancies are identical, even to the same woman. Some women manage to float through the 9 months with nary a whisper of nausea or a burp of heartburn. Others begin throwing up before the stick turns blue and are still heaving as they're wheeled into the delivery room. Twenty years ago, symptoms that were simply too annoying—sore backs and legs from standing all day at work, or extreme fatigue—would have led many women to quit their jobs (often at the urging of their employers). Now that the law mandates more support and accommodations for pregnant women, most are able to continue working right up until their due dates.

While that's good news, it does mean that a symptom you once might have handled in the privacy of your own home (nausea, or excruciatingly itchy skin, for example) is now something you have to deal with on the job. And while you might initially think that a symptom like insomnia has nothing to do with work, you realize it has *everything* to do with work when you find yourself asleep at your desk or dozing off in the middle of a staff meeting. Other symptoms, like morning sickness, can be more of an issue at work, where you may have to walk (or run) halfway around the building to get to the bathroom, than at home, where the bathroom is mere steps away and there are far fewer people to see you running.

Never fear. There are ways to minimize the disruption that even the most debilitating pregnancy symptom can have on your job. Before I tell you how, I have to start with a caveat: The alphabetical list below is by no means an exhaustive rendering of every pregnancy-related annoyance, ache, and pain. Instead, it's intended to provide a job-oriented focus on pregnancy-related health. As such, the list highlights just the conditions that could affect your work. Finally, neither this book nor any other should substitute for individualized care from a health care provider familiar with your personal medical history and needs.

Note: Throughout this chapter, a small cross (✚) is used to highlight symptoms that may signal a potentially serious disorder. If you experience any of these symptoms, contact your health care provider immediately.

Absent-mindedness. A.J., 37, executive secretary to a bank president and 7 months pregnant, sometimes thinks she's losing her mind. "I'm known for my organizational skills. I remember everything—where I put this, who is responsible for that, the names of all my coworkers' kids," she says. "But these days I feel like my head is in the clouds and I can't remember a thing. It's like the baby has hijacked my brain." Feeling spacey and forgetful is a classic, almost stereotypical, hallmark of pregnancy. Whether it's typical of pregnant women in general is still questionable. One study of pregnant

Pregnancy 911

These symptoms, at work or at home, warrant an urgent call to your health care provider:

* Sudden, unexplained leg pain
* Swelling in hands and/or face
* Severe headache
* Visual disturbances, such as blurred vision
* Persistent vomiting or unexplained diarrhea
* Vaginal bleeding or spotting
* Any gush or leakage of fluid from the vagina
* Unexplained vaginal cramping
* Cessation of fetal movements after they have become regular
* Falls and other accidents
* Fainting

women in India, however, found the women had lower levels of certain neurotransmitters—chemicals that help to relay messages among brain cells. These changes were associated with minor and temporary impairment in memory, most notably during the second trimester.

But take heart—new research debunks the long-held notion that a pregnant woman is a space case. Researchers at the University of Sunderland in the U.K. have found that although pregnant women rate themselves as being more forgetful and spacey than they were prior to becoming pregnant, they really aren't. Pregnant women given tests of memory and concentration actually performed no differently from a non-pregnant comparison group.

Even if your neurotransmitters are working fine, fatigue and stress alone are enough to make you forget things and feel distracted. Try to get enough sleep and follow the suggestions on coping with stress in chapter 6.

If you feel that you're forgetful and having trouble remembering things (regardless of whether you really are), make use of lists on paper or on your PDA. Keep a pad and paper next to your bed to capture those ideas and that to-do list swirling around in your head so you can relax and sleep better, knowing they won't disappear overnight. Your PDA or computer can be set up (ask the nearest 14-year-old how, if you're not sure) to sound a chime or alarm when it's time to get ready for the next meeting or leave for your prenatal appointment. Finally, rely on some version of the string-around-the-finger technique. Shelly, a 32-year old technical writer, typically wears a stack of silver bangle bracelets on her left wrist. When she found that she often forgot whether she had taken her daily prenatal vitamin after breakfast, she began putting one of the bracelets on her right arm in the morning when she got dressed, and moving it to its usual spot after she'd taken her vitamin.

✚ **Accidents and falls.** Sandra, a 33-year-old accountant, was standing on a small stepstool to reach a bookshelf in her office when she lost her balance and fell. "I guess I should have known better than to climb up there—I'm 6 months pregnant," she admits. "But I'm short, and the book I needed was on the top shelf." Fortunately, neither Sandra nor her baby suffered any harm beyond a bruised ego (hers, not the baby's), but her story isn't unusual.

A shift in your center of gravity as your baby grows, coupled with hormonal changes that bring loosening of joints and ligaments, increases the likelihood that you'll find yourself off balance during your pregnancy—more prone to bumping into things and falling. Add the fact that you may be chronically tired, and that, after a point, you probably can't see your feet anymore, and you can see why it's time to start stepping carefully.

Fortunately, fetuses are pretty well protected in their cozy package of maternal bubble wrap. Most moms and their babies survive these common scrapes and spills with no ill consequences, but check with your physician if you're at all concerned, and definitely call if you've been involved in any major accident, such as a car accident, even if you think you're fine. Also call your health care provider if you have any of the warning signs listed in "Pregnancy 911" on page 89 after a fall or slip.

The best way to protect yourself against falls, however, is to prevent them. Wear flat or low-heeled shoes, take extra care on wet or icy surfaces, don't stand on chairs or ladders, and cultivate some tall friends who can reach things for you.

Aversions. Pregnancy's hormonal changes often bring with them a heightened sensitivity to certain smells and tastes. That doesn't mean that you can ask the other 30 people who work with you to give up their espresso machine, or the woman in the cubicle next to yours to go easy on her trademark perfume. You *can,* however, control your immediate environment. Many pregnant women give up perfumes and scented lotions or cosmetics for the duration, skip the coffee (even decaffeinated), and take their meals alfresco instead of in a steamy lunchroom. If you have your own office, open the windows or keep a small fan at your desk to blow away offending odors. If not, make sure you take a few fresh air breaks during the day. Most aversions pass as your pregnancy progresses.

Back pain. Pregnancy-related backaches come in several varieties and stem from several causes. Neck and shoulder aches most likely result from tension and/or the increased weight of your growing breasts. Both upper and lower back pain can result from changes in the distribution of your weight, which stresses your spine, back, and abdominal muscles. The hormones of pregnancy also relax your ligaments and lead to other changes in your back, abdominal muscles, and joints—all necessary so your body can accommodate the growing baby even as it prepares for labor.

Lower back pain that extends or shoots down one buttock and into one leg is probably sciatica, caused when the baby's head compresses the sciatic nerve. "Sciatica is uniquely painful, easily the most troublesome symptom I experienced during my pregnancy," says Mei, a 41-year-old university art teacher who delivered her first child at age 40. "I did take some comfort in knowing it wasn't really dangerous to either me or my baby, but—ow! It's so hard to find a comfortable position with sciatica."

✚ If, however, your lower back pain is coupled with an overall sense of malaise, blood in your urine, and/or a mild fever, you may have the beginning of a kidney infection. Call your physician as soon as possible.

Otherwise, for upper back and neck pain and discomfort, try stretching regularly. Try setting the clock on your computer to beep at you every 30 minutes to remind you to stretch. And make sure your bra has wide, supportive shoulder straps. You can purchase inexpensive padded strap wideners at most lingerie shops. And drinking a cup of hot herbal tea, or taking a brief walk, can help unkink any stress-related knots.

For aches in your lower back (once you and your doctor have ruled out any possibility of an infection), try one or more of the following:

* Stand up straight. Are you allowing the baby's weight to pull your tummy too far forward? Tuck your belly in as you walk or stand, and wear comfortable flat or low-heeled shoes.

* Put your feet up. If you're lucky enough to have an office door, close it and prop 'em right up on your desk or a chair. If not, get a small stool and make good use of it.

* Belt it. A maternity belt—a wide, soft, supportive elastic band that wraps around your lower back and under your belly—can take over part of the job of tired, stretched abdominal and back muscles as it cradles the weight of your growing baby. These can be found in maternity wear shops and catalogs, particularly those that carry active wear for pregnant women.

* Go for pain relief. Ask your health care provider if you can take some acetaminophen (Tylenol or its generic equivalent) to alleviate aches.

* Stand right. If you stand a lot at work, try bending forward very slightly (taking care not to throw your hips forward or let the baby's weight pull you too far forward) and standing with one foot slightly elevated on a low stool or footrest. If standing becomes too stressful as your pregnancy progresses, speak to your employer about accommodations to keep you working: a chair or stool at your workstation, or, if necessary, a temporary reassignment to a less physically taxing position.

* Go for heat. If the warmth doesn't bother you, try a microwavable heating pad or one of the new, chemically generated heating pads available at drugstores. (Some are custom-made to fit the lower back area and can be worn under your clothes).

* Stretch for sciatica. *Gently* try to stretch your back, arms, and legs, and try moving into different positions. This may help, although it can sometimes make the problem worse. Ask your doctor what you can take for the discomfort. And hang in there: When your baby moves over a little—and he will, eventually—the problem will go away.

+ **Blood clots.** Pregnant women and those who have recently given birth have an elevated risk of developing blood clots known as deep vein thromboses, or DVTs. These can be dangerous if one breaks lose and travels to your lungs, where it can cause a fatal condition called pulmonary embolism. So if you have any unexplained pain or swelling in your legs, shortness of breath, or wheezing, call your doctor immediately. Also let your healthcare provider know during your first prenatal exam if you have a personal or a family history of DVT.

You can help prevent blood clots by maintaining a reasonable weight and engaging in regular exercise. Being stationary for too long can increase your risk of DVT. Make sure you get up and move about at least once every 45 minutes or so if you're in a long meeting or sitting at your computer. Make frequent stops on long car trips as well.

Colds and flu. With everything else a pregnant woman has to cope with, it seems you ought to have a doctor's note to excuse you from run-of-the-mill illnesses like colds and flu during your pregnancy. Sorry. Pregnancy doesn't convey any immunity from the cold your husband brings home from the office, or the stomach bug that's making the rounds of your preschooler's classroom. If you do get sick, check with your doctor before taking any over-the-counter medications. Most are safe for use during pregnancy, but it never hurts to double-check. And don't forget home remedies. Hard candies (butterscotch is especially good) may relieve a dry throat or a mild cough as effectively as cough drops or medicated cough syrups. Warm showers, hot tea, and a humidifier can relieve nasal congestion, while gargling with salt water can soothe a sore throat.

Constipation. Constipation is a common but not inevitable problem during pregnancy. It's caused by (what else?) hormonal changes—increased levels of progesterone can make digestion sluggish—and by the growing weight of your uterus and its 9-month tenant. Constipation may also be a problem after you deliver. There's the understandable reluctance to tax tired, sore muscles with a bowel movement (especially if you've had an episiotomy). Constipation can also be exacerbated by having more sedentary days than you might be used to, and the fact that your body is rerouting fluids to produce a steady flow of milk.

The solution in both situations is to get plenty of healthy fluids—read: water. You might also try prune juice (or, the politically correct term these days: dried plum juice). Grandma was right: it works, and some brands even taste pretty good. A diet rich in fruits, vegetables, and whole grains is also essential—you'll be amazed what a regular (no pun intended) breakfast of oatmeal with a handful of raisins or chopped apples can do. Warm drinks also help many women. (Try heating your prune juice in the microwave for a few seconds.) And don't be embarrassed to ask your doctor or midwife for a stool softener (not a laxative) to use for a few days until you're feeling like yourself again. Do *not* take laxatives or mineral oil-based preparations. These can contain harmful chemicals and are simply too strong (and too unpredictable in the timing of their—um—outcome) for safe use at the office or at home.

Cravings. Aversions to food and odors are typically a bigger problem at the office than cravings are, but both can be a pregnancy-related pain. And although you won't be taking most of your meals at work, you may have fewer food options available during these hours, and thus be more vulnerable to giving in to cravings that may not serve your (or your baby's) nutritional needs. The folk wisdom about them is that our cravings signal nutritional deficits in our bodies, but more pregnant women get the urge for cheeseburgers and hot fudge than for liver and broccoli. Most research discredits the notion that we crave what we're lacking nutritionally, so don't let too many cravings lead you down the road to Chunky Monkey ice cream. To cope with the mid-morning desire for a corn dog and pickles, keep a drawer in your desk stocked with more nutritious options. If you'd give your baby's inheritance for a candy bar, for instance, try substituting a healthy sweet like raisins or dried apples. If potato chips are calling your name, try to assuage your cravings with lightly salted, whole wheat pretzels.

Dizziness and fainting. In the movies, an episode of fainting is what often tips us off to the heroine's pregnancy. In real life, fainting is rare during pregnancy, but occasional episodes of dizziness are common, particularly during the second and third trimesters when the growing uterus may press on blood vessels causing your blood pressure to drop.

Alert your doctor if you have an episode of fainting. She will probably want you to come in for a quick check. Because low blood sugar can also contribute to feelings of dizziness, eat frequent, small meals and have a healthy snack if you feel yourself getting light-headed. Keep naturally sweet snacks, like raisins and other fruit, in your purse or desk. When you get up from lying or sitting down, stand slowly to avoid the "head rush" and dizziness that can come with changing blood pressure. Hormonally related fluctuations in

your body's thermometer can also make you feel hot and woozy—
some fresh air and a cool drink usually helps. If you really feel like
you're going to faint, lie down with your feet elevated or sit and bend
at the waist with your head between your knees.

Emotions. "My coworkers call me Crying Charlie," says Maggie,
a 26-year-old pediatric nurse nearing the end of her first trimester.
"I'm happy that I'm pregnant, but everything makes me weepy—sick
kids, well kids, cute newborns, crabby parents, the copy machine not
working—you name it."

As Maggie's story illustrates, a pregnant woman's emotions can
change faster than the weather thanks to fluctuating hormones.
Maybe you're like Maggie, a walking river of tears. Or maybe you're
worse than Oscar the Grouch on Sesame Street, snapping at everyone
from the mail clerk to your boss. The good news is that it's probably
temporary. As the hormonal surges level off in your second trimester
and morning sickness and fatigue abate, your energy will probably
peak. You'll feel healthy, sexy, and more emotionally grounded; and
because miscarriage is much less likely at this stage, fears that may be
fueling your emotional fires should dissipate. Of course, your mileage
may vary—every woman's experience is different.

Until then, take good care of yourself. Getting enough sleep and
eating well can make you feel more grounded. But also pay your emotions some serious attention. Some are fleeting and changeable at this
stage, but if you find yourself persistently angry, ask yourself if there's
a reason and if there's anything you can do to change the offending
situation. If your weepiness seems to signal a real depression (or if you
have a history of depression), speak with your doctor about treatment
options that are safe during pregnancy.

In general, though, there's nothing really wrong with being a
little more emotional unless it unnerves your co-workers or embar-
rasses you at staff meetings. Take a few breaths or break away from

Exercise: The Best Medicine

Years ago, pregnant women were urged to rest and relax while they were waited on hand and foot. No more. For most women, exercise is as important a part of pregnancy as prenatal vitamins. Plus, physical activity—even just a daily walk—can help with nearly all of the pregnancy-related problems listed in this chapter. The benefits include:

* Healthy weight control
* Muscle fitness that can increase stamina, make labor and delivery easier, and help you recover faster
* Natural mood and energy enhancement
* Prevention or improvement of heartburn, insomnia, constipation, headaches, and swelling

Some types of exercise are not appropriate because of pregnancy-related changes in your balance, joints, ligaments, or muscle tone, or because of risks inherent in certain sports. Most doctors advise pregnant women to avoid bicycling (including stationary bikes), horseback riding, rappelling, boxing, and gymnastics. Swimming, yoga (make sure your instructor knows you're pregnant so she can help you avoid any potentially dangerous positions), running, walking, and low-impact aerobics are generally thought to be safe for healthy pregnant women. But check with your doctor before beginning or making any changes to your exercise

the action if an intense situation threatens to bring on tears (you can always slip out of a stressful meeting on the pretext of having to pee—again!). Keep your pocket full of tissues and learn to dab discreetly at your tear-filled eyes.

Fatigue. Hannah, 30, is a dedicated graduate student in physics, but 2 weeks before her due date she fell deeply asleep during a lecture on string theory, right in the front row of class. The student next to her discreetly tried to nudge her awake, but the sympathetic professor program during pregnancy. If you were exercising regularly before you got pregnant, discuss whether your current program is still appropriate.

If you're new to exercise, start slowly. Warm up with careful stretches (avoid pointing your toes because this can bring on leg cramps), and cool down with more stretches afterward to ward off muscle soreness. Also drink plenty of water during and after exercise. And when the workout's over, avoid hot tubs and saunas which are unsafe during pregnancy because they raise your core temperature.

✚ Stop exercising immediately and call your doctor if you experience any of the following:

* ✳ Shortness of breath
* ✳ Dizziness or fainting
* ✳ An accident or fall
* ✳ Vaginal bleeding, rupture of membranes, or uterine contractions
* ✳ Overheating
* ✳ Vomiting

You will probably be advised to limit or avoid exercise if you have pregnancy-induced hypertension, a weak cervix, premature labor, a history of late miscarriage, persistent bleeding or spotting, or a preexisting condition that could make exercise hazardous for you or your baby.

stopped him. "Let her sleep—she's pregnant! She needs all the rest she can get," the professor said. He was right. For while pregnancy may satisfy one part of your biological clock, it can wreak havoc on the part related to sleep.

During the first trimester, you may feel like you're constantly sleeping, or sleepwalking. This is normal. Your body is burning lots of energy to create that new person. The second trimester is typically a period of greater energy and alertness, but your sleepiness may return, like Hannah's, as you near your due date and it becomes harder to get enough sleep at night.

The National Sleep Foundation reports that four out of five women have trouble sleeping during pregnancy. There are lots of reasons. Hormones, difficulty finding a comfortable position, vivid dreams, and the need to go to the bathroom several times at night—an urge triggered by the baby's pressure on your bladder—all add up to a sleepless night. Whatever the cause, fatigue can definitely interfere with your on-the-job performance.

If your fatigue is extreme, ask your doctor to test you for anemia, or low blood iron, a common condition during pregnancy. Also, nap when you can. Some offices these days actually have designated nap rooms. If yours doesn't, you might be able to get a few minutes of shut-eye in your car during lunch, or behind your closed (and locked) office door. Alternatively, get moving. A 20-minute walk during lunch can be as refreshing as that nap. If your job permits, get up and walk around a little, or stretch at your desk, at least once every 45 minutes. And if you feel your eyelids drooping, have a cold drink, splash your face with cold water, or brush your teeth; the fresh, clean feeling makes some women feel more alert.

If you're having trouble finding a comfortable position at night, try sleeping on your side. Most doctors advise sleeping on your left side for improved circulation. As your pregnancy progresses, sleeping on your belly will be next to impossible anyway and sleeping on your back is not advised because the weight of your uterus can interfere with the flow of blood to your heart. Use pillows to make yourself more comfortable: a slim one under your belly, a firm one at your back for support, a medium-sized one between your knees to improve circulation and add support.

If your sleep is disrupted by heartburn or acid reflux, elevate the head of your bed very slightly by putting a stable, 2-inch board under the feet or supports at the head of the bed (at first it might feel as if you're going to slide off the end, but you'll soon become accustomed to the arrangement). Some women find they sleep better in the later months of their pregnancy if they give up their bed and sack out on a comfy sofa or reclining chair. Regular exercise should also improve your sleep as well as boosting your energy level during the day. Don't get too frantic about late-pregnancy insomnia; some suggest this wakefulness is good practice for the middle-of-the-night feedings soon to come. And unless your doctor recommends it, stay away from sleeping pills or other medications designed to induce drowsiness. Some are potentially harmful to your developing baby, and even those that may be safe can stay in your system a long time, adding persistent drowsiness to the fatigue you already have.

Fears. Fears during pregnancy are normal, but can be exacerbated at work for several reasons. The most common one is that someone in your workplace insists on telling you horror stories about her high-risk on-the-job pregnancy, or his wife's cousin's hairdresser's poor little baby and what happened because she stayed on the job too long. Take another look at chapter 4 for ways to deal with these breaches of etiquette (and lapses in compassion).

The earliest stages of pregnancy can feel as though they are fraught with peril. We all know or know of women who have miscarried, or developed unpleasant or potentially dangerous symptoms during pregnancy. Remind yourself that these cases are the exception, not the rule. Appoint a good friend to feed you regular doses of reassurance and good cheer and say things like "97 percent of all pregnancies turn out just fine, you know." By your second trimester, when you're past the stage of pregnancy that feels the most fragile and when your prenatal tests have all come back negative, your anxiety should subside to a manageable level. But if you find you simply can't stop worrying and obsessing over your fears, especially if they're interfering with your work or other daily activities, talk to your doctor.

Gas. It happens to everyone from time to time, but pregnancy increases the likelihood you'll experience these times more often. It's one thing when it happens at home, but at the office? Again, blame those hormones for changing normal digestive patterns.

To prevent embarrassing flatulence, exercise, drink plenty of water, and ask your doctor to recommend an over-the-counter antacid (bonus: most of them are cheap and rich in calcium). Also, avoid foods known to be gas triggers: broccoli, cucumbers, radishes, onions, carbonated soft drinks, and, of course, beans.

Headaches. Headaches during pregnancy are not at all uncommon and may be caused by several things. Hormonal changes (again) may make tension headaches more likely, although ironically, if you regularly suffer from migraine headaches, you may find these are less frequent or disappear altogether during pregnancy. Pregnancy-related worries and stress can also contribute to headaches, as can lack of sleep.

Acetaminophen is probably your first line of defense, especially if you're at work and away from your relaxing bathtub. Most doctors agree that a little caffeine is safe during pregnancy; a cup of tea or a caffeinated soft drink (not the super-caffeinated ones like Mountain Dew) can sometimes stave off a headache before it gets too painful.

Hunger and low blood sugar can also bring on a headache, so frequent small meals may help. If you simply can't get away from the office for a meal, try keeping nutritious snacks—granola bars, fruit, rice cakes, pretzels, and juice boxes, for instance—in your purse or desk (see "Your Pregnant-on-the-Job Tool Kit," opposite). If your headache persists or worsens, or comes on very suddenly and intensely, call your doctor.

Your Pregnant-on-the-Job Tool Kit

Keep these items on hand at work to help you cope with pregnancy symptoms on the job:

* Nausea-fighting snacks (pretzels, oyster crackers, saltines, and so on) and ginger ale
* Toothbrush, toothpaste, and mouthwash (for cleansing your mouth after nausea or vomiting)
* Wet wipes (for freshening up)
* Extra pair of support hose
* Antacids (doctor-approved)
* Acetaminophen (Tylenol) for minor headaches
* Bottled water
* Lotion or cream for dry skin and itching
* Sanitary pads in case of mild incontinence or spotting
* Motion sickness wrist bands
* Doctor's or midwife's phone number and insurance information
* A go-with-anything extra blouse, in case nausea or excessive perspiration get the better of your clothes

Heartburn. "Heartburn was the only pregnancy symptom that gave me any trouble," says Janet, 28, a food writer for a big city newspaper. "But man, I had it in spades! In my job, of course, I eat often and I eat a lot of different things. I pretty quickly figured out, though, that I needed to try to avoid more than a little taste of the spicy things I love best. And anything greasy was just plain out." Heartburn results as your expanding uterus puts pressure on your stomach, while hormonal changes can make the problem worse as increased levels of progesterone slow digestion and relax the valve that normally acts like a sort of firewall between your stomach (where acids belong) and your esophagus (where it doesn't).

Janet's survival kit contains a good antacid, and yours should, too. Your health care provider will probably approve over-the-counter antacids that work in the stomach without affecting the rest of your body (or your baby). If heartburn is a persistent problem, enlist the help of gravity by sleeping on a couple of pillows or elevating the head of your bed about 2 inches. (Place a board under the feet at the head of your bed.) Avoid tight clothing, lying down after eating, large meals, eating too quickly, spicy or fatty foods, chocolate, peppermint, and any other foods that trigger or intensify your symptoms.

Heat. Don't be surprised if you begin to feel like your thermostat is permanently set on high. Your basal metabolic rate, which helps to keep your body temperature steady, is about 20 percent higher than it was before you got pregnant. In the winter, this is not such a bad thing—you may find, for instance, that you don't need a heavy coat—but in the summer it can be brutal, especially if your workplace isn't air-conditioned.

To cope with temperature extremes, dress in layers. If you have to wear a suit, make your blouse a sleeveless shell so you can slip off your jacket for some instant air conditioning. Stick to natural fibers such as cotton and silk—they breathe better than polyester and rayon. If you can control the thermostat in your personal office, fine, but don't insist that your non-pregnant coworkers adjust theirs to suit you. Instead, get an inexpensive personal-sized fan for your desk. Because you'll probably perspire more, make sure you're bathing regularly, and wear plenty of deodorant. Drinking cold water and juice to stay well hydrated can also help. Try keeping a half-filled bottle of water in the freezer at work, then topping it off with cold water and sipping the icy liquid at your desk.

Hemorrhoids. Varicose veins of the rectum and surrounding tissues are all too common in pregnancy. They can be caused by straining during bowel movements, or simply by pressure from the growing baby. Hemorrhoids aren't dangerous, but there are few things that can make you feel more miserable, especially if your job involves long hours of sitting (though, frankly, standing isn't so great, either). Even if you make it to the end of your pregnancy hemorrhoid-free, you're not out of the woods yet. Many women congratulate themselves on making it through pregnancy without them, only to develop hemorrhoids from pushing during labor or from post-delivery constipation.

The best way to avoid hemorrhoids (see above) is to avoid constipation, exercise, drink lots of water, and head to the bathroom as soon as nature calls. If you already have hemorrhoids, try warm baths before and after work to ease discomfort, and sitting on a doughnut cushion—a nifty little circular pillow that you can buy at most pharmacies. Do not use prescription or over-the-counter remedies for hemorrhoids without consulting your doctor. Most hemorrhoids disappear without medical intervention after you deliver and begin to eat and exercise more normally.

Morning sickness and nausea. "I was actually anxious to gain a little weight with my first pregnancy because I wanted to look, as well as feel, pregnant," says 22-year-old Mindy, a cardiology research assistant for a large medical school. "Instead, I had such terrible morning sickness that I actually *lost* weight during my first 2 months of pregnancy. Also, handling lab samples made me feel so ill that my supervisor finally let me switch to some computer-oriented tasks until I stopped throwing up."

Wouldn't it be great if morning sickness (sometimes called NVP, for nausea and vomiting of pregnancy) only occurred in the morning? Then you could get the day's unpleasantness over with instead of having to cope with it at work, too. No such luck. For most women, "morning sickness" is a misnomer, as the nausea of pregnancy continues throughout the day. And most women will experience it; about two-thirds to three-fourths of pregnant women get "morning sickness" in some form. Hormones (of course) are responsible, but low blood sugar has also been implicated. Findings of a recent study conducted at Oxford University suggest that morning sickness, which is often triggered by greasy or fatty foods, may prevent the pregnant woman from consuming too many fat calories that might interfere with the development of the placenta.

Regardless of the cause of morning sickness, there are many potential remedies that may alleviate or prevent it. If morning sickness bothers you at any time of the day, try some of these nausea-busting tricks:

* Avoid tastes and smells that may trigger nausea.

* Sip ginger ale (strong ones seem to work better than the grocery store brands—ask the clerk at your natural foods store to recommend a spicy one) or hot ginger tea throughout the day. To make the tea, cover about a tablespoon of freshly chopped or grated ginger root with boiling water; steep for 6 to 8 minutes, strain, and add a little honey or sugar to taste.

* Try motion sickness bands like Sea Bands. Research has found this noninvasive, do-it-yourself acupressure technique to be remarkably helpful and completely free of side effects.

* Use a little do-it-yourself acupressure. *Gently* press on a spot at the center of the underside of your wrist, about three finger-widths below your palm (just where the motion sickness band would apply pressure).

* Eat five or six small meals a day instead of three larger ones.

This will allow you to keep something in your stomach at all times without overloading it.

* Stock your office fridge or desk drawer with light, healthy snacks and nibbles: yogurt, rice cakes, pretzels, fruit.

* Have a light snack before bed.

* Keep crackers at your bedside, nibble a few when you wake up—before you get out of bed—and then wait 15 to 20 minutes before rising.

* Eat bland, lightly salted foods: crackers, a baked potato sprinkled with salt, pretzels.

* Take your prenatal vitamins after eating. These can sometimes cause nausea if taken on an empty stomach.

* Avoid motion sickness or other nausea medications (even herbal or "natural" ones) unless you have your doctor's okay.

Shortness of breath. As your baby grows, it gradually crowds all the space within you, leaving less room for various organs like your lungs. This, in turn, can lead to shortness of breath, especially during the third trimester.

Feeling breathless can make you feel panicky, so try to relax. Breathe as slowly and as deeply as you can, slowing your activity at the same time. If you're exercising when shortness of breath occurs, stop and cool down, breathing slowly. Slow, steady breathing before giving a talk or presentation at work can also help to keep your breathing steady.

✚ In rare cases, shortness of breath can indicate a serious problem, such as a blood clot. If symptoms worsen or persist, or occur early in pregnancy when your uterus isn't that large, contact your doctor.

Swelling. You're not only eating, sleeping, and breathing for two, you're also carrying enough blood and water (some of it in the form of amniotic fluid) for two. This can lead to swelling in your feet and ankles (a condition called edema), especially as you near your due date. Particularly hot days may also bring on swelling. Additionally, pressure from your growing uterus may also trap blood in your lower extremities and force fluid into your tissues, causing swelling.

Ironically, making sure you drink enough water is the solution. Staying well hydrated can improve circulation and keep fluids from pooling in certain parts of your body, like your ankles. Also, try to elevate your feet whenever possible. At work, slide a second chair up to your desk, either beside you or across the desk from you, and prop your feet on it. And try support hose, which work by compressing your ankles and legs, thus counteracting the internal pressures that force fluids into your tissues and trap them there. Put them on in the morning before you get out of bed for maximum benefit. Other remedies include exercising and avoiding salty foods.

✚ Report any extreme swelling, or swelling in your face and hands, or swelling accompanied by visual disturbances or headaches, to your doctor right away; this may signal the onset of preeclampsia (hypertension during the latter stages of pregnancy).

Urination. Any woman in her third trimester can tell you the location of every bathroom in every shop, restaurant, library, and office within a three-county area. Frequent urination is caused by the pressure the expanding uterus puts on your bladder, leaving little room for urine. So when you gotta go, you gotta go, even at work. This isn't, in and of itself, a serious problem, but it can be annoying and inconvenient. The worst part is that getting up at night to hit the bathroom adds to the sleep deprivation you're probably already feeling.

To limit the waterworks, avoid caffeinated beverages, which can

Kegels: The Secret Exercise That Will Change Your Life

Kegels are an exercise to strengthen the muscles you'll use during delivery, which happen to be the same muscles that can help guard against urinary leakage and stress incontinence (peeing a little when you sneeze, cough, laugh, or run). They're easy, quick, and can be done anywhere, anytime.

To do a Kegel, clench or contract the muscles in your pelvic floor area, the ones supporting your bladder, urethra, rectum, and uterus. You can locate the correct muscles when urinating: They're the ones you use to stop the flow of urine. Do 20 to 30 Kegels several times a day for maximum benefit. Can't remember to do them? Train yourself to "Kegel" every time you sit down at your desk, whenever you stop for a red light in your car, or while waiting in line.

As with any exercise, be patient. It may take several weeks before you notice a difference. And don't stop once you deliver the baby. Continuing to strengthen these muscles can speed your recovery after delivery. It can also make sex more enjoyable for both you and your partner—an added benefit. And Kegels are one of the best ways to ward off problems with incontinence as you get older.

have a diuretic effect. Do *not* cut back on fluids, however, but try to drink less in the evenings. If you're having trouble with slight leakage when exercising, laughing, or sneezing, wear a lightweight sanitary pad. Faithfully doing Kegel exercises can make a big difference in controlling this problem. (See "Kegels: The Secret Exercise that Will Change Your Life" above for instructions on how to do this valuable exercise.) If you weren't doing them before you got pregnant, start now—it's never too late.

KEYS TO KEEPING
THE BALANCE

✖ Hormonal changes or the growing weight of your baby, or both, can be blamed for nearly every pregnancy-related symptom.

✖ Every pregnancy is different. You may experience many symptoms, a few, or almost none at all.

✖ While you can't prevent many symptoms of pregnancy, exercise plays a key role in keeping some of the more annoying ones to a minimum.

✖ Eating a healthy diet may also help with several pregnancy-related symptoms—that means plenty of fruits, vegetables, and other high-fiber foods, coupled with lots of water.

✖ Call your health care provider *at once* if you experience any of the warning signs of potentially dangerous illnesses or events listed on page 89 or those marked with a cross (✚) within the text.

6

WORKPLACE STRESSES AND HAZARDS DURING PREGNANCY

Carmen, 26, had worked in a large dry cleaning shop for 3 years before she got pregnant. "I had headaches all the time," she says. "I can't say for certain that they came from the chemicals we used to clean the suits and dresses, but they made me nervous. Still, I might have gone on working there for a few more years—it was a good job, with nice people—if I hadn't gotten pregnant. Suddenly I felt as if I were getting headaches for two, and I started to worry about whether the chemicals and odors could harm the baby I was carrying. My boss said he didn't feel that there was any danger, but because the smells were making me sick, he let me transfer to the company's billing office, which was in another building. I don't know whether my fears were well grounded, but I do know that my headaches went away, and I delivered a healthy baby boy."

As Carmen discovered, pregnancy can open your eyes to all sorts of hazards, both on and off the job, that you may not have even been aware of pre-pregnancy. The most important thing—beyond any paycheck, promotion, or title—is the safety of you and your baby. So read on to learn how you can identify and then address any potential health hazards both at home and at work.

DANGER—WOMEN AT WORK

The effect that hazards in your environment have on your developing baby is a complex function of your genetic background (some people seem to be more susceptible to certain toxins) and the degree to which you're exposed. But it's the nature of the specific hazard that most determines the potential danger to you and your baby. Make sure you tell your health care provider what kind of work you do and the conditions under which you do it. If you don't know whether the materials you work with are dangerous, talk to the person in your company who is responsible for OSHA (Occupational Safety and Health Administration) compliance. A fairly large company may have a safety department responsible for these and related issues; in a smaller company, it might be your human resources director. If you're part of a collective bargaining unit, your union representative may also be able to help.

Here's a brief catalog of some fairly common workplace hazards, along with some potential outcomes.

Alcohol. As noted earlier, and as you must have heard from your health care provider by now, there's no definitive threshold for safe levels of alcohol consumption during pregnancy. Crossing that line, wherever it is, is strongly associated with a constellation of anomalies and defects known collectively as Fetal Alcohol Syndrome, or FAS. These children generally have small heads, joint problems, congenital heart defects, mental retardation, and/or facial abnormalities. So stick to club soda at the company holiday party, and save the champagne for the birth (if you're not nursing).

Animal hazards. If you work with animals (as veterinarians,

The Critical Period

The type of damage that can occur in a fetus exposed to a toxic substance depends on the time of exposure. Developing embryos go through what are called "critical periods," which are narrow windows during which organs, systems, or tissues develop. If exposure occurs during a critical period, that organ, system, or tissue can be irreparably damaged.

For instance, children with fetal alcohol syndrome (FAS) have characteristically wide-set eyes, while children exposed to rubella (German measles) during the first trimester of pregnancy are often blind. In both cases, the damage occurred during a relatively narrow window when the eyes are developing and facial features are maturing.

Likewise, exposure to rubella can cause devastating malformations or even miscarriage if it occurs during the first trimester, which represents a critical period for organ development. However, rubella is less damaging later in pregnancy.

farmers, researchers, and those who work in kennels, stables, pet shops, zoos, and animal shelters do) be aware that critters, their waste, and their surroundings may carry E. coli bacteria, tularemia, toxoplasmosis, histoplasmosis, and other disease-causing agents that can have implications for your child's development.

Toxoplasmosis, for instance, which is associated with cats and their waste, causes only cold-type symptoms in the mom, but can result in miscarriage, stillbirth, or brain and eye defects, hearing loss, and cognitive disorders in the fetus. E. coli can be transmitted both through the consumption of undercooked beef and through the petting or handling of farm animals. E. coli can not only sicken you, causing severe kidney problems, but can also be passed to your baby, who can develop diarrhea, fever, and even meningitis shortly after birth. Little is known about the effects of tularemia (also known as "rabbit fever," since contact with rabbits and the parasitic insects that feed on them can transmit this disease) on pregnant women, but the powerful antibiotics used to treat it have not been approved for use during pregnancy.

Bottom line: Get someone else to clean the litter box, the bird cage, the rabbit hutch, and muck out the Augean stables. Avoid direct contact with these animals (E. coli, for instance, has been transmitted to children and parents at petting zoos) and their surroundings. If this isn't feasible, ask to be reassigned to other duties until after your baby is born. In the meantime, don't pat the bunny.

Caffeine. The coffee machine is a staple in workplaces the world over. But before you reach for your next cup of joe, know that research on the effects of caffeine consumption during pregnancy is mixed. Even decaffeinated coffee may not be totally okay, since some studies suggest the chemicals used to decaffeinate coffee may contribute to birth defects. Overall, though, the general consensus is that small or moderate amounts of caffeine are safe. Avoid high-caffeine drinks like some of the currently popular super-caffeinated soft drinks, and high-test coffees. Tea, which has 40 milligrams of caffeine per 8-ounce cup (compared to coffee's 100 milligrams per 8-ounce cup), may be a better choice. But be sure to avoid any herbal tea or drink containing tansy (check the ingredient list on the label), which can cause spontaneous abortions.

Computers. As soon as she learned her daughter was pregnant, Sheila's delighted mother gave her daughter the family's heirloom christening dress, a dozen pink roses (she's hoping for a granddaughter), and a special screen purported to diminish exposure to extremely low frequency electrical fields to attach to her computer at work. "It's supposed to protect me from harmful rays coming from my computer, but it makes me look like I'm expecting aliens to land at my desk," laughs Sheila, 29. "Still, it did prompt me to ask my midwife whether spending so much time at the computer could hurt me or my baby, and she told me not to worry about it."

As personal computers and laptops became commonplace in homes and offices, concerns like those expressed by Sheila's mother have become common, too. But numerous studies conducted on the issue have found no strong evidence linking computer use to miscarriage, birth defects, or any other pregnancy-related risk.

Environmental hazards. Workers in a tremendous variety of jobs come into contact with potentially hazardous chemicals. This includes chemists, those in the medical, dental, and pharmaceutical fields, painters, house or office cleaners, farmers and horticulturists, dry cleaners, pest control technicians, carpet cleaners, and many others. Listing all hazardous substances encountered in workplaces—and their possible risks for you and your child—is beyond the scope of this book, so you must do a little legwork.

Fortunately, chemical manufacturers are required by law to provide material safety data sheets on the hazardous materials they produce or import. If you work with a hazardous material, your employer must make these data sheets available to you. Look under "health effects" on these sheets for information on known reproductive hazards.

Also be vigilant about reading labels on products you use at home and at work. You can look up questionable products on the Internet, and talk with your health care provider and your OSHA officer at work about any concerns you have. The OSHA Web site, at www.osha.gov, offers office safety information on specific hazards and on the regulations pertaining to workplace safety. OSHA's site can also link you to their nearest regional office. In addition, OSHA's offices can be reached by telephone at (800) 321-OSHA.

Handle any suspect materials with care, taking all possible precautions. If you have concerns about how safe a product or other material is, or about any activity you are asked to perform at work, express your concerns to your supervisor, union representative, or

(continued on page 118)

Tips for Airplane Travel

Women who travel for business (or pleasure) often wonder whether they can safely fly throughout their pregnancies. Generally, you're safe up until your 36th week, which is when most airlines (and doctors) bar you from flying. You should also stay on the ground if you have spotting, bleeding, or, of course, contractions. Some airlines may even require a doctor's note if you're planning to fly any time during your third trimester.

It's not that air travel is inherently dangerous for pregnant women, although long flights can increase your risk of blood clots. This reluctance to allow women in the late stages of pregnancy to fly is largely a precaution against the need for an emergency landing if the woman goes into labor.

If you do fly during pregnancy, early or late, you'll be safer and more comfortable if you observe the following advice:

Pack smart. Carry essential medical records, your health care provider's number, and information about locating emergency care at your destination (the name and number of someone your healthcare provider recommends, if possible).

Investigate your destination. Travel to high-altitude areas (in which the air is not as oxygen-rich) is not advisable during pregnancy. The Centers for Disease Control and Prevention (CDC) advise women in the first or second trimester of pregnancy to stay below 4,000 feet above sea level; women in their third trimester should limit their destinations to places no higher than 2,500 feet above sea level. If you're traveling to a foreign country, check travel advisories relating to health issues. The CDC maintains an up-to-date Web site listing their health-related travel advisories at www.cdc.gov/travel/. These listings are accompanied by information about recommended vaccines (check with your own physician to find out whether these are safe during pregnancy) and include a special section on traveling while pregnant or breast-feeding.

Stay regular. That means getting plenty of fiber, fluids, and exercise to ward off constipation.

Buckle up. But put your seat belt under, not on top of, your belly, and make sure it's snug, but not too tight.

Fly right. Stick to larger airplanes with pressurized cabins.

Move around. Pregnancy coupled with the sardine-like environment of most airplanes these days sharply increases your risk of developing blood clots. Make sure you get up whenever possible and walk around the airplane, even if it's just to go to the bathroom. If you can't walk around the plane, do leg and ankle exercises in your seat (try writing the alphabet in the air with each foot—but don't point your toes or your calves may cramp).

Perform flight checks. Of your body, that is, and alert a flight attendant immediately if you develop leg pain or shortness of breath, both possible symptoms of a blood clot.

Choose a travel-friendly outfit. That means comfortable clothing and shoes, and dressing in layers to compensate for your stuck-on-high thermostat.

Drink. Since the air inside planes is very dry, drink plenty of water. Dehydration can cause Braxton Hicks contractions, little practice contractions that do not signal the onset of genuine labor, but that can be uncomfortable nonetheless. Also maintain a steady blood sugar level with nutritious snacks, and avoid caffeine, which can contribute to dehydration.

Be prompt. Arrive early for check-in so you can pre-board at your leisure and pick a seat near a bathroom, particularly if you're flying an airline that doesn't use assigned seating. Also request an aisle seat when making reservations, for easier access to the bathroom and more leg room for exercising.

Pick the right meal. If your flight has meal service, request a vegetarian or kosher meal. Because these are provided only upon request, they tend to be fresher and prepared with more care than standard airline fare.

Pack for the flight. Take along bottled water, small snacks, and an inflatable pillow for back support. Suitcases should be light, rollable, and, when possible, carried by someone else.

Pamper yourself. Use all available conveniences—airport shuttles from your parking lot, gate shuttles, and other services as needed.

OSHA officer. Remember that the Pregnancy Discrimination Act contains provisions requiring your employer to make the same accommodations for you as would be made for any employee with a disability, so you may be able to get your employer to shift you to a position in which you are not required to handle unsafe materials.

Food. Unless you're a restaurant reviewer or a chef, you may not be doing a lot of eating *for* your job, but most of us do eat *on* the job. Whether it's a working lunch in a five-star restaurant or a quick consultation over a hot dog at the corner stand, moms-to-be must be aware of potential food hazards. These include listeria, a bacterium typically found in processed meats such as hot dogs and cold cuts; E. coli, which may be found in unwashed fruits and vegetables and their unpasteurized juices, or in raw and undercooked meats; and salmonella, which is associated with undercooked poultry and eggs. Listeriosis has been associated with premature delivery and stillbirth, E. coli and salmonella with digestive and infectious disorders soon after delivery in babies whose mothers were affected during pregnancy. So pass on the steak tartare at that business lunch, put the sushi and swordfish on hold, and stick to pasteurized fruit juice. If you travel in countries where bacterial and viral infections are a perennial problem, eat only fruits and vegetables you can peel, and—to use the cliché—don't drink the water (unless it's bottled or you can guarantee it's been boiled). That means avoiding ice, too.

Nicotine. Chemicals carried in cigarette smoke cross the placental barrier, increasing the level of carbon monoxide and depriving the developing brain of oxygen. This can harm your baby in numerous ways: low birth weight, prematurity, stillbirth or miscarriage, higher rates of Sudden Infant Death Syndrome (SIDS), hyperactivity, and a higher rate of respiratory infections during infancy. In fact, a recent British study found that women who smoked during pregnancy increased their risk of having a stillborn baby by 28 percent.

Even if *you* don't smoke, the smoking others do around you can still harm your baby. Exposure to secondhand smoke in pregnant women has been linked to an increased risk of lung disease, asthma, and other problems for baby and you.

Physical stressors. Occupations involving heavy lifting, long hours of standing or sitting, or any job requiring impeccable balance or working in high places can bring discomfort or even potential dangers for you and your baby. Teachers, day care workers, flight attendants and railway conductors, mail and package carriers, dancers and dance teachers, and yoga or martial arts teachers should be aware of these issues. Physical stressors you encounter during your recreational activities should also be taken into consideration.

Joy Ann, 26, had never taken ballet as a child, but had always wanted to. When the gym where she exercised after work offered an adult beginners' ballet class, she signed up immediately. "One night toward the end of my first trimester I jokingly commented that I'd soon have to buy a maternity leotard. The teacher, who hadn't known I was pregnant, kindly but firmly insisted I had to quit the class. Pregnancy hormones, she told me, can affect muscles, ligaments, and joints in such a way that injuries can occur more easily if they're overstretched or stressed during exercise. She was very nice about it and referred me to a friend of hers who teaches a special yoga class for expectant moms, but I was chagrined to have to put my dreams of taking a ballet class on hold again."

In 2001, rresearchers at the University of Michigan Medical School in Ann Arbor reviewed 29 studies of the effects of physical stressors in the workplace on pregnancy outcomes. They concluded that there is a very real relationship between physically taxing activities on the job and an increased risk of premature labor, delivering a low birth weight baby, and high blood pressure or preeclampsia. Remember that the Pregnancy Discrimination Act requires that your employer make reasonable accommodations to keep you safe from workplace hazards during your pregnancy. These might be as simple as providing you with a chair in which to sit if standing all day is too taxing, or as comprehensive as reassigning you to a less hazardous position within the company for the duration of your pregnancy.

Radiation. The genetic material of either parent can be damaged by repeated exposure to x-rays or dangerous chemicals. This is why, for instance, pregnant women should not have routine x-rays taken at dental appointments, and why protective shields are used to cover your reproductive area when you do have an x-ray if there's any possibility you might be pregnant. Massive doses of radiation can cause fetal death; smaller doses have been associated with a number of mental and physical abnormalities. Medical and dental employees, as well as baggage screeners, may be at risk here and should consider a job reassignment during their pregnancy.

Viral hazards. This category is of greatest concern to those who work in medical settings: doctors, nurses, physicians' associates, or support staff in hospitals or clinics (even receptionists). You're also at risk if you work in child care settings, schools, inpatient facilities for children, and camps because you are often exposed to numerous childhood illnesses, many of which pose only a minor annoyance for the child but can be devastating for your baby. Avoid exposure to children who have, or who have been exposed to rubella, chicken pox, cytomegalovirus (CMV), and fifth disease (sometimes called "slapped cheek" disease for the characteristic redness it gives to cheeks). Flu viruses can, in rare cases, cause birth defects if the exposure occurs during the first trimester. If you work in such settings, ask your health care provider about your potential risk. In most cases, having a particular illness, or having been inoculated against it, will protect you and your child.

STRESS, STRESS, AND MORE STRESS

Taylor, 34, has a poster over the desk in the office from which she runs her own small communications business. "Don't tell me to relax," says the phrase under a picture of a frazzled-looking cat. "It's only my tension that's holding me together." The same could be said of Taylor. She thrives on her high-responsibility, high-pressure, deadline-driven job. But as she neared the beginning of her third trimester of pregnancy, she felt worn out, anxious, and crabby. On top of her pregnancy fatigue and worry over how she'll keep the business going during her leave, her largest client told her he's considering hiring someone in-house to do the work he currently contracts to her. Then there's her really big concern: She recently learned her mother has breast cancer. Too stressed to cook after work, she and her husband have been eating a lot of take-out food. If he's working late, she just snacks on ice cream instead of eating dinner.

There has never been a pregnancy that didn't bring with it a certain measure of stress and anxiety, particularly for women who work outside the home. "When I'm thinking about how great motherhood will be, I start to get anxious about how I'll be able to continue working," says 29-year-old Carrie. "When I think about how much I love my job—I'm an on-air host for a jazz radio station—I can't imagine how I'll ever be able to give my baby the attention and love it will need. And don't even get me started on how we're going to afford this baby or what we're doing for child care when my leave is over!"

A study commissioned by CIGNA Health Care and the March of Dimes found that 65 percent of pregnant women worry about the effects of their stress on their own health and that of their babies. The March of Dimes also says that maternal stress is likely to be an important factor in the statistic that one in eight babies is currently born prematurely. It's enough to, well, stress you out.

STRESS AND YOUR BABY

When you experience problems or uncertainties—worrying abut the outcome of your pregnancy, a preschooler with the flu, a report due too soon at work, a job you hate, marital difficulties, a squabble with a friend, financial problems—you're experiencing stress. Your body reacts physically, going on high alert as if it were in mortal physical danger. Chemicals called stress hormones flood your body to provide a sense of alertness and readiness either to fight a perceived source of danger, or to flee (the so-called "fight-or-flight" response). Among other functions, these chemicals instruct your body to send more oxygen-rich blood to your muscles, away from your internal organs. Your respiratory rate and adrenaline levels increase, and your heart rate skyrockets. All of this is well and good if you are Bruce Lee about to fight an army of enemies, or an antelope preparing to escape from a hungry and determined lioness. But if you're a woman with a family to care for, work to get done on the job, and, of course, a baby on the way, being held in thrall to these stress hormones for long periods of time is exhausting and upsetting—not to mention potentially dangerous to your baby.

Remember the discussion of pregnancy-related symptoms in chapter 5? We blamed nearly everything from morning sickness to rashes to heartburn on the hormonal changes you're experiencing. Well, stress only exacerbates these changes, making the resulting symptoms even more unpredictable. The potential effects of these changes on your developing baby are unclear. But the more we learn about the nature and function of stress hormones, the more concerned researchers become about the negative effects they can have on both you and your baby.

For instance, medical researchers at the University of California in Los Angeles call stress the second most important cause (after relevant medical factors) of low birth weight and prematurity in infants. One reason, researchers suggest, may be that, like Taylor, women under prolonged or extreme stress don't take as good care of themselves. Often, they don't get enough sleep or eat a healthful diet.

Stress may also rob your baby of oxygen and nutrients. When you're stressed, your body releases the stress hormone epinephrine, or adrenaline. This is the same chemical that makes your heart race, your breathing quicken, and leaves you feeling agitated and upset when

Stress Hormones and Your Baby

Your stress directly stresses out your unborn baby. In a 2003 study, scientists from Greece and Tufts University in Massachusetts found that women whose babies are born prematurely have higher blood levels of a stress hormone called corticotropin, which is secreted by the brain in response to stress.

Other research demonstrates that stress hormones can have a direct effect on the ways in which your baby's developing brain is being formed. Persistently high concentrations of stress hormones can be toxic to the developing brain, interfering with the rich connections—the lines of cognitive and emotional communication—among brain cells. Infants thus exposed before birth and in the earliest months of life are, in a sense, hardwired to have more difficulty handling stressful conditions. This in turn has been found to be related to a number of problems in early childhood, including increased aggression, difficulty with concentration and self-control, memory impairment, and trouble establishing a healthy and mutually satisfying relationship with others.

Does this mean that a few stressful days on the job will wreak havoc with your baby's development? Not at all. Most problems of this sort are seen in cases of extreme stress (such as might occur in an abusive relationship). It does indicate, however, that there is not only a link between our emotional environment and our health, but also between our own stress and our baby's health. Doing what you can to minimize your exposure to stressful situations, or to cope with and compensate for them in healthy ways, will benefit you and your little one.

something stressful occurs. But as epinephrine levels rise, the blood supply to the uterus and placenta drops. This, in turn, may cause uterine contractions, possibly sending you into premature labor.

A stress hormone called corticotropin (CRH) may also signal the release of histamine-like chemicals (the ones that cause allergy symptoms). Early in pregnancy, high levels of these chemicals can lead to disruptions in the formation of the placenta, causing miscarriage. CRH has also been found to play an important role in regulating the onset of labor—it's been nicknamed "the placental clock" because it seems to tell your body when labor should begin. If these levels get out of whack, you could go into labor too early.

By increased understanding of the effects of stress on pregnant women and their babies, researchers hope they can get better at identifying women at risk for stress-related miscarriage or early delivery, and develop ways to prevent these problems.

What Is Low Birth Weight?

Low birth weight refers to the circumstance in which an infant's weight at birth is low in proportion to its gestational age. As a medical standard, an infant born weighing less than 2,500 grams (about 2½ pounds) is considered to be low birth weight. These babies are at risk for both physical and cognitive developmental problems related to oxygen deprivation at birth. They may also have slow rates of growth and typically require considerable monitoring and medical intervention, usually including time spent in the newborn intensive care unit.

The long-term consequences of low birth weight can be significant: These children are at risk for neurological problems and also have difficulty regulating their emotions and responding appropriately to others. Low birth weight babies may also be both lethargic and difficult to calm, which can be frustrating to parents trying to soothe or connect with their newborns.

STRESS AND BLOOD PRESSURE

The additional fluid and blood volume of pregnancy usually keeps your blood pressure low. If stress makes your blood pressure rise, however, your risk of "pregnancy hypertension," or preeclampsia, also rises. Preeclampsia is characterized by high blood pressure, protein in your urine (one of the things doctors look for when they test your urine during prenatal visits), headaches, swelling, and visual problems.

As your blood pressure rises, a corresponding drop in oxygen delivered to your tissues can affect your baby because the placenta can't supply adequate levels of oxygen and nutrients to the fetus. Left untreated, this may develop into full-blown eclampsia, which can lead to fetal death as the mother experiences seizures and sometimes coma. Fortunately, most women with pregnancy-related hypertension who receive regular prenatal care get treated in time to prevent life-threatening eclampsia.

Being overweight, drinking alcohol, and smoking increase your risk of developing preeclampsia. Also make sure your healthcare provider is aware of any history of hypertension. Preeclampsia may develop suddenly toward the end of your pregnancy; if the risk of eclampsia is high enough, you may need an early delivery by cesarean section to safeguard both your baby's health and yours.

STRESS AND BRAIN DEVELOPMENT

Women who are chronically stressed or subjected to acute (sudden) stress have an increased risk of depression. And that, in turn, can affect your baby. Research suggests that women who are chronically depressed tend to have infants who are difficult to soothe and comfort.

For decades, psychologists assumed this was because severely depressed moms were unable to attend and respond adequately to the cues of their infants, resulting in behavioral problems in their babies. But advances in brain research and biochemistry suggest that stress in the mother might actually reshape the developing brain in the baby. Infants of depressed moms contain higher-than-normal levels of the stress-related hormones cortisol and epinephrine. Essentially, these babies may be hardwired to be more susceptible to stress after birth.

SUDDEN, PRONOUNCED STRESS

In her 12th week of pregnancy, Marcia, 36, received a call at work telling her that her 7-year-old son, who was carpooling to school with her neighbor, had been in an accident. As she raced out of work to make the long drive to the hospital, she knew only that he was alive but unconscious, and in critical condition. After 3 days in intensive care, when it was finally clear that their son would make a full recovery, Marcia and her husband slept for the first time since the accident. The next day, Marcia had a miscarriage.

Can stress actually cause birth defects or miscarriage? Some researchers believe it can. Animal studies find that if levels of the stress hormone cortisol suddenly increase, the offspring are more likely to be born with birth defects. And in humans, doctors note that sudden, extreme stress early in pregnancy—such as that caused by the death of a child—is associated with birth defects, including those of the lip, palate, or heart.

Scientists speculate that extreme and sudden increases in stress hormones in the mother's body during the early stages of pregnancy may affect developing tissues in the embryo. Researchers stress, however, that given the low overall risk of birth defects (about 3 to 4 percent), even the increase of severe stress brings that risk up to only about 5 percent.

None of this is designed to stress you out. Rather, the goal is to impress upon you the potentially negative consequences of stress on you and your baby so you'll be more likely to find ways to reduce the stress in your life, or at least moderate the way you react to it. Read on for some healthy ways to manage stress.

MANAGING YOUR STRESS

Avoiding stress completely is probably an unrealistic goal. Learning to avoid more serious and pervasive forms of stress, though, is an important part of taking care of yourself and your baby. Until doctors and researchers can sort out what it is about stress that can be so damaging—chemical imbalance? the tendency of stress to make us slip up when it comes to taking good care of ourselves?—the key to better mom and baby health lies in learning how to manage the way you react to stress so you don't get those sudden or prolonged spikes in stress hormones. Here's how.

Expect it. Into each pregnancy a little stress may fall. Don't let worrying over stress become an additional stressor. Keep in mind that we all have varying levels of stress at different times, and the overwhelming majority of babies are born healthy and ready to love and learn. Don't let undue concern over the possible effect of an annoying incident or bad patch at work make you even more tense.

Explore healthy ways to cope. Carol, 27, was pregnant when terrorists struck the Pentagon and the World Trade Center on September 11, 2001. "I had quit smoking when I found out I was pregnant," she says, "but it was all I could do during the days and weeks following the tragedy not to reach for my cigarettes again. Then I compensated for not being able to smoke by overeating for a while, but I realized that wasn't doing my baby and me any good, either. So every time I wanted either a cigarette or a candy bar, I reached for my knitting instead. I even took a little knitting project to work with me and did a few rows every day on my lunch break. Not only was it incredibly calming, but by the time my daughter was born, she had a great wardrobe of little sweaters and caps."

Follow Carol's example and find healthy ways to comfort yourself when you're feeling stressed: Rent your favorite old movie, reread a book you love, bake some whole wheat bread, write in your journal. Stuck at work? Use your break time for a quick walk or 10 minutes of yoga, add to your list of possible baby names, or close your office door and sip a cup of tea. Do what you can to avoid stressful news and images, too. If world events are stressing you out, take a news break—ban newspapers and television and radio news for the duration.

Find support. You're not alone. Talking with other pregnant women who may be experiencing the same types of stress you are can be a big help. The Internet offers scores of pregnancy message boards and mailing lists, many of them arranged by due date, so you can correspond with women in the same month of pregnancy. These women often maintain contact after their babies are born and get each other through a whole new set of stresses. (Can you say "colic"?)

BabyCenter.com, ePregnancy.com, and many individual service providers like AOL (type in the keyword Parenting) offer message boards of this type, as does virtually every pregnancy-related Web site (check the appendices of this book). Even many maternity wear companies offer message boards on their Web sites (again, check the appendices).

Take a time out. Spend a few minutes every morning before work, or in the evening when you get home, taking a walk or simply sitting quietly, meditating or engaging in creative visualization. Any activity you enjoy can also help to banish stress: Garden, read, cook something healthy, or meet with your book group.

Meditation and Pregnancy

Practiced for thousands of years by adherents of religions including Buddhism, Christianity, Judaism, and Islam, and embraced over the past half-century by many secular philosophies as well, meditation is gaining the respect of modern science for its ability to calm the mind and relieve stress.

Many businesses now even offer meditation instruction and a quiet place for a meditation break to their stressed-out employees. They cite improved health, diminished stress, and increased creativity as outcomes. Recent brain research indicates that meditation can lower blood pressure and heart rate, relieve stress, and help to diminish irritation and anger. Cheap and portable (no equipment is required, beyond a place to sit and perhaps a cushion), meditation can be done virtually anywhere.

There are many different kinds of meditation, but most fall into one of two groups: Those in which the meditator focuses on her breath, an image or symbol, or a word or phrase, and those in which the goal is to concentrate on compassion or other positive emotions. For more information on the many kinds of meditation, take a look at the references in the appendices of this book, or check out Internet sites such as www.mindandlife.org, www.dailyzen.com, www.beliefnet.com, or www.imeditate.com.

Exercise. Exercise is a great stress buster. A recent University of Miami study, among others, cites both fitness and mental health benefits of exercising during pregnancy. This holds true both for women who were already active, and those who didn't exercise much prior to becoming pregnant, as long as they started slowly. Women who exercised had greater aerobic fitness, energy, and stamina. Research has also shown that exercise can help to relieve depression. As noted earlier, make sure your health care provider signs off on any exercise regimen. And if you take antidepressant medication, do not change your regimen without a physician's close guidance.

Call In Reinforcements

If stress reaches the point at which you believe it's affecting your health or interfering with your ability to take care of yourself, call your health care provider, a counselor, or someone from your office's confidential employee assistance program (if you have one). Extreme sadness or anxiety, feelings of guilt, a marked inability to sleep that goes beyond what you might expect from pregnancy, unusual changes in appetite, a significantly decreased energy level, or an inability to take pleasure in the things you usually enjoy may indicate you're suffering from depression. Discuss these problems with your doctor as soon as possible. She will help you regain your footing and return to the point at which you can take care of yourself and derive pleasure from your pregnancy.

Let someone else take care of you. Lean on your husband or partner, your best girlfriend or your mom for support and a little extra TLC during this time.

A LITTLE REASSURANCE

Sometimes when you're pregnant it seems as if everything from the neighbor's cat to a kiss from your virus-ridden young niece, to the carpet cleaner used in your office presents a minor (or major) hazard. How can any fetus be expected to develop into a healthy baby if the world is full of paint thinner, second-hand (and first-hand) cigarette smoke, radiation, mercury-tainted swordfish, car exhaust, ozone-depleting aerosol propellants, extremely low frequency electrical fields, and reality TV?

Relax. As noted before, the rate of birth defects in the general population is relatively low, about 3 to 4 percent. This means the overwhelming majority of babies turn out just fine. The odds are strongly in favor of your baby being fine, too.

KEYS TO KEEPING
THE BALANCE

Workplace hazards come in many different forms, including environmental toxins, biohazards, and physical stressors. Be proactive in working with the person in your company who is responsible for OSHA (Occupational Safety and Health Administration) compliance. This person can help you identify any potential hazards at work and help limit your exposure to them. Also remember that the Pregnancy Discrimination Act mandates that your employer make reasonable accommodations to keep your work area free of hazards.

Severe or persistent emotional and psychological stress has been linked to birth defects, miscarriage, and premature birth.

Protective factors such as adequate rest and sound nutrition, social support, exercise, and stress reduction techniques can be highly effective at reducing stress and its negative outcomes during pregnancy.

7

DRESSING FOR TWO

Benjamin Franklin probably wasn't thinking about pregnancy when he wrote, "Beware of ventures which require new clothes." At what other time in your life are you going to have such a legitimate excuse to shop? Pregnancy brings a virtual mandate to re-outfit yourself from head to toe. For some of us, putting on that first maternity dress or pair of slacks carries with it a strong sense of validation. Finally, you have visible proof the baby is real. For instance, Alice, 25, a speech therapist, says she almost felt as if she were playing at being pregnant until the day she wore her first maternity clothes. "Putting on the 'uniform' of maternity clothes somehow made it all more official," she recalls.

Maternity wear options are amazing today. Look back at the photos of your mom or grandmom, when they were pregnant. In the dark ages of pregnancy wear, the emphasis was entirely on hiding as much as possible of you, and of your little passenger. Any trace of sexuality or sensuality would have been considered improper, if not downright obscene. So maternity dresses were designed with yards of fabric in the style of Omar the Tent Maker, cut to cover you from earlobes to shins with an emphasis on draping—not unlike the way one uses a sheet to cover furniture in a house

133

that's going to be closed up for months. Ruffles and bows served to both infantilize you and to distract anyone from evidence that you might have been—gasp!—sexually active. Most toddlers' sunsuits didn't sport as many ruffles as the clothes these mature women were expected to wear. Remember, you're *having* an infant, not turning into one.

Today, thanks to some hip designers (many of whom have gone through their own pregnancies) and the consumer power pregnant women represent, we've gone from camouflage to couture. Maternity clothes are streamlined and sexy, practical, and so much more fun to wear. Many stores in which you happily shopped pre-pregnancy offer maternity lines of their own.

You can even find maternity workout clothes, which are a far cry from the leggings paired with the oversized T-shirt stolen from her husband's closet that many a pregnant woman had to make do with a decade ago. And instead of two or three styles, there are dozens, as designers and manufacturers of maternity wear have awakened to the fact that a woman's individual sense of style doesn't shrivel up as her belly expands.

"When I had my first baby about 6 years ago, I was most comfortable in fabrics and garments that draped over my tummy," says Carlin, 33, a professor of mathematics. "I didn't go out and buy caftans and muu-muus, but I wanted some coverage, so I bought long sweaters and roomy dresses I could move in. At the same time, though, I thought my basketball tummy was beautiful—so did my husband. Now that I'm pregnant again, I'm glad there are other choices. I love the new maternity wear that emphasizes, rather than hides, what I'm carrying. I'm not quite up to a bare midriff, but I think the women who can pull it off look fantastic. I feel so sexy when I'm pregnant—why shouldn't I be allowed to *look* sexy, too?"

YOUR BODY, YOUR LOOK

Whether you work in a conservative Wall Street setting in which suits and pumps are *de rigeur*, or in a more laid-back workplace in which every day is "casual day," you probably started to think about maternity clothes minutes after sharing the happy news with the baby's father. Whether you thought, "Yes! This is going to be so much fun!" or "Darn! Now I have to wear maternity clothes!" probably depends on how you feel about your body.

For instance, Mackenzie, 28, an oncology nurse, admits she was never on the best of terms with her body. "I was always a little uncomfortable in my skin," she says. "Nothing really extreme, but nothing terrific, either. But almost from the beginning of my pregnancy, it's like I've discovered this physical part of me for the first time—and I like the way I look and feel. When I think of all the amazing things my body's doing right now, I just want to dress it up and take it out on the town! This is the first time in my life I've paid much attention to my clothes. Now I just want to buy myself beautiful things."

Tanya, a 38-year-old executive assistant for a law firm, isn't quite so confident about her changing body. "I don't think I'm the bare-belly type," she says. "I like clothes, but I hate to shop, and I work in such a conservative office that buying maternity clothes isn't all that fun. I mean, once you have a tweed skirt, a plain wool skirt, and a jacket, what else do you need?"

Quite a lot, as it turns out.

LET'S GO SHOPPING

Before you fire up the charge cards and head to the mall, sit down and do a little planning. The first thing you need to consider is your workplace. Conservative or funky? Casual Fridays or casual everydays? Do you need clothes for in-the-office days and clothes for out-with-a-client days? Maybe you need to entertain clients at dinners or parties. Maybe there's an office picnic coming up. Day at the races? Night at the opera? Got a wedding in the offing? Your pregnancy wardrobe needs to be as versatile as your pre-pregnancy one. But as big an event as pregnancy is, it's also time-limited. And in just a few months, those great new duds you bought are going to be relegated to the back of your closet. So it's not worth blowing the baby's college fund (or the money you're saving for your leave) on dozens of smart outfits. Now, more than ever, you need to plan a wardrobe for comfort, functionality, suitability, and seasonality.

WHERE TO SHOP

Every mall has at least one specialty maternity shop, and many more general stores (including the upscale discount store Target) have maternity departments. If you're an Internet shopper, you can't beat the convenience of virtual maternity stores. The Internet is also a great place to purchase those hard-to-find items such as supportive maternity bras for sports, or sexy lingerie that will grow with you. In Appendix E on page 243, you'll find a list of terrific online outlets for maternity wear.

If you're more comfortable with bricks than clicks, most maternity shops offer a few special advantages, including oversized dressing rooms and "belly pillows" to help you visualize how a garment will look and fit as your tummy expands. Most important, a good maternity wear shop will be staffed with salespeople knowledgeable about the kinds of changes you can expect in your body as your pregnancy progresses. They can offer invaluable advice about maternity wear for different occasions, and about how to make the transition from one stage of pregnancy to the next.

DO'S AND DON'TS OF MATERNITY CLOTHES

Before I discuss what to look for in specific garments, here are some tips on maternity wear in general.

DO keep your own style and comfort level in mind. If you weren't comfortable in rhinestone studded sweatshirts pre-pregnancy, don't buy one now, *especially* if it has a gilt arrow pointing at your belly and "BABY" embroidered in pink and blue floss.

DON'T be afraid to try something new. Maybe you've always steered away from horizontal stripes because your mother told you they make you look fat. When else are you going to get a chance to wear them?

DO dress your age. This is the most wonderfully grown-up time of your life. It's not a time to start dressing like Britney Spears, or, worse, Angelica from *Rugrats*. Beyond merely avoiding ruffles and bows, focus on beautiful fabrics, simple, clean lines, and styles that emphasize your best assets.

DON'T dress in the past. Avoid the high-collars, tent dresses, ruffles and bows your mom (or grandmother) wore, unless you happen to be the keynote speaker at an *I Love Lucy* fan convention.

DO stay current. Because you're going to be wearing maternity clothing for only a limited time, this may be the one opportunity you'll have (until your next pregnancy, anyway) to buy what's trendy. After all, if it's out of style in a year, you won't want to wear it anyway.

DO buy quality, feel-good clothes. You're going to be wearing these clothes a lot, particularly if you can afford only a few pieces.

DO buy machine washable. Who wants the expense of dry-cleaning? Beyond that, consider your personal ecosystem: The odor from the chemicals used in the dry-cleaning process may make you nauseous, not to mention they're probably not very healthy for you or the baby. Make sure, however, that the clothes you choose can stand up to repeated washings. If you do have to dry-clean some garments, air them out well before wearing them; and unless you use a pick-up-and-deliver dry-cleaning service, ask someone else to drop them off and retrieve them for you.

DO buy at the right time. "The first thing I wanted to know was when I could start wearing maternity clothes," says Jillian, 26, a portrait photographer. "I'm kind of a clotheshorse anyway, and I just couldn't wait." Most women who are pregnant for the first time find they need maternity clothes around their 4th month. Your timing may vary, of course: Every body reacts differently to pregnancy. If you're especially slender, you may be able to wait a little longer. If you take eating for two a little too seriously, you may need new clothes sooner. And if this isn't your first pregnancy, you will probably need maternity clothing earlier than you did the first time around. "By the time I had my fourth child," says Sandra, 40, the mayor of a small midwestern town, "my body seemed to know precisely what to do and what shape to assume. I had to get out the maternity clothes practically the morning after I'd conceived!"

There are some tricks you can try to bridge the gap between the time your regular clothes stop fitting and when you're ready for maternity clothes (usually toward the end of your first trimester). For instance, slip one end of a rubber band or hair elastic through the buttonhole of your pants or skirt and loop both ends around the button. Top with a waistband-covering shirt or sweater, and you can sail through a couple of weeks in comfort.

Jackets, too, can expand your options as you make the transition to maternity clothing. Worn over a dress, skirt, or pants, jackets lend legitimacy to separates. And they don't have to button, affording the option of wearing your pre-pregnancy jackets throughout much of your pregnancy. Try knit jackets, which provide the warmth of a sweater with the class of a jacket. Remember, too, that your accessories still fit. Use them to get more mileage out of these pre-pregnancy transitional clothes.

DO pace yourself. If you buy everything you think you'll need while you're still in your 4th month, you may find yourself with nothing that fits right as your third trimester progresses. You may also, by that point, be bored silly with everything in your closet. Re-

The Price-Conscious Gal's Guide to Maternity Clothes

On a budget? Consign yourself to consignment or thrift shops. Since maternity clothes are worn for a relatively short period of time, these are great places to find beautiful, barely worn items. Then when you're finished with them, take them back to the same shop for a bit of return on your investment. Just be sure to check for tears, stains (particularly under the arms), missing buttons, and so on.

Other tips for the cost-conscious pregnant gal:

Less is more. It's easy to overbuy. Start with a few items and add pieces as you need them. It's impossible to tell at the outset how big you will get, or whether an unusually cool spring will let you continue to wear the items you bought in the winter.

Always a borrower be. Borrow from your friends, steal from your sisters. Graciously accept offers of maternity wear from friends and relatives who no longer need the clothes, and fill in your wardrobe with great white shirts or oversized sweaters you snitched from your partner. Even if they're too big for office wear, using these items during your time off enables you to spend a little more on work clothes. For big-ticket, short season items like coats, look in consignment shops.

Think long-term. Buy garments you'll still want to wear after you deliver. Remember that for a few weeks after birth, you'll still look like you're 4 or 5 months pregnant, until your uterus returns to its pre-pregnancy shape. Clothing that's adjustable (either with buttons or ties, or with comfortable elastic panels or waistbands), in fabrics with some give—matte jersey, soft knits, microfibers—will see you through those first few postpartum months. Make sure any blouses and shirts you plan to wear post-pregnancy open down the front or have hidden slits for nursing, if you're planning to breastfeed.

member you'll be wearing most of your maternity pieces again and again. Designate a little of your wardrobe budget to buy yourself a wonderful item or two each month throughout your pregnancy. When you think you'll scream if you have to put on that black shift one more time, a fabulous shirt to wear under it or jacket to wear over it can get you through the crisis.

DO focus on your best features. If you've got it, flaunt it. Pregnancy is a great time to show your best stuff. We're not talking Frederick's of Hollywood here, just a little strategic maximization of your assets. Feel completely dumpy as you expand? Take advantage of the wonders pregnancy can work on your hair and skin (more on that further along) by playing them up with a great cut and flattering makeup. Making the most of the features you love can help you to look better—and to feel better about your overall look.

THE GOLDEN RULES OF MATERNITY WEAR

Creating a maternity wardrobe is a breeze if you follow these three basic principles:

Buy in bulk. Several companies offer coordinating basics, usually in black: a sleeveless jumper, a pull-on skirt (buy a long one and a short one), a pair of slacks, a shell or tee, and a jacket. Buy these in quality fabrics, such as a matte jersey knit or lightweight wool crepe, that can stand up to abuse and span the seasons.

Stick to neutrals. Black is just a suggestion, of course. It looks great on everyone and goes with everything. But beige, brown, or forest green can work just as well.

Complement like crazy. Now add color and texture. With a background of neutral and simply shaped basic garments, adding complementary pieces expands your wardrobe exponentially. For instance, add a tailored collar shirt, a turtleneck, a tee-shirt, and a sweater jacket to those initial pieces you bought, and you'll have at least 25 outfits to wear—at least 5 weeks worth of dressing with no repeats. Add an elegant dress, a pair of slacks in a different cut or color, and a stack of tees in bright or spicy colors and you can make it until your due date without wanting to burn anything.

SECRETS OF THE STYLISH AND EXPECTING

When it comes to selecting clothes that make you look—and feel—good while you're expecting, there are a few additional secrets you'll need to know. Among these are how to find the right fit for your growing body, and how to select savvy options for special occasions. You'll also need to understand the importance of high-quality undergarments, and—because no one feels good when their feet are aching—learn how to make smart choices in footwear.

FIND THE RIGHT FIT

As noted earlier, don't try to buy bigger non-maternity clothes to bridge the gap between your pre-pregnant wardrobe and your maternity clothes. Maternity wear isn't just bigger. Clothing for pregnant women is cut differently to fit right and to make room for growing bellies and breasts. Also, quality maternity clothes grow with you. For instance, pants may come with a stretchy front panel, a fly front with an elastic panel in the back of the waistband, elastic side panels on either side, or an all-over stretchy fabric that fits either at the natural waistline or under the belly.

Similarly, maternity sweaters and blouses, like dresses, are designed to hang more attractively once you've grown a little. So don't worry if the hems look slightly off-kilter when you first try them on, hanging a bit longer in the front than in the back.

DRESS ME UP, DRESS ME DOWN

In some ways, dressing up during pregnancy is easier than dressing down, with numerous options for formal and semi-formal wear. Consider what you'll need before you shop: Do you have a wedding to attend in your 8th month? Do you entertain clients in the evening or attend lots of cocktail parties? You don't need a different dress for each event. A simple black dress can be accessorized and customized with scarves, jewelry, a satin jacket, to fit nearly any occasion.

You need to pay just as much attention to casual office wear as to evening wear, however. Leggings and the oversized sweater borrowed from your partner's closet will just look sloppy.

If you can wear jeans to work, you're in luck: Manufacturers are finally making them in wonderful colors, cuts, and fabrics for pregnant women. Look for trims, cuts (straight-legged, flare-legged, or cropped), patterns, and colors that are hot when you're buying. Fabrics with a little spandex provide more stretch and greater comfort without resembling your great-grandma's polyester pants.

Even if every day is casual day at your workplace, you may not want to stick with jeans all the time. Soft trousers in flannels or knitwear in cooler months, or cotton or linen in the summer and spring keep you from crossing the line from casual to grungy. Pullover sweaters or knit tops that are a step or two up from tee-shirts work well, too. Even if you've never been fond of dresses, you may find that an informal dress—perhaps an overall-style jumper or a cozy sweater dress with no confining waistband— is more comfortable and carefree during pregnancy than your favorite pants, and can be dressed up or down to suit the occasion.

BUILD A SOLID BASE

It may seem ironic, but it's worth investing a large portion of your wardrobe budget where it won't show: your undergarments. Buy the best bras and underpants you can afford.

Pick the right panties. Here again, fashion is finally on the side of the mother-to-be. You can now find styles you'd like even if you weren't pregnant. Lace, leopard-skin, and every racy color imaginable are available, as is every cut. If you were a thong girl before, you can continue to be one in specially cut maternity thongs. Briefs and bikinis are available in cuts kind to growing bellies, as are waist-high panties in traditional or high-legged styles.

Fabric is the main consideration here. Now more than ever, you want panties that are comfortable, soft, breathable, and hold up in the washer. Buy the nicest cotton you can afford—pima cotton is especially soft and comfortable, though a little pricey. Elastic should be wide and soft, and seams should be minimal—some cotton knit panties now have completely seamless sides.

Bring home the right bra. Maternity bras are probably the most important pieces of clothing you can buy during your pregnancy. A high-quality, comfortable, properly fitting bra makes your clothes look and fit better, and leaves you infinitely more comfortable. So this is one shopping stop where you definitely don't want to scrimp. Go to a reliable department store or lingerie shop and have a proper fitting. (They won't charge extra for it.) Maternity stores also sell maternity bras, and the sales clerks will know how to fit them correctly. Expect to spend a pile here, anywhere from $25 up. Buy at least three, one to wear, one for the drawer, and one for the laundry. If you're exercising regularly, get two or three maternity sports bras as well.

Your breasts are one of the first parts of your body to grow with your pregnancy. So if you want to wait before you invest in maternity bras, try a "bra extender," a short length of lingerie elastic fitted with hooks and loops to widen the back of your regular bra. Similarly, inexpensive strap cushions can take some of the weight off your shoulders as your breasts grow heavier. Both of these items can be found in lingerie and maternity shops.

Soon, though, you'll need the extra features of a real maternity bra: more support, wider straps, and extra provisions for adjusting the fit as you make the transition from Kate Moss to Dolly Parton. Supporting your breasts during pregnancy can make a difference in how much sagging you have afterwards, especially if you are large-breasted. You may want to begin to wear a bra or a supportive camisole even at night, more for your own comfort than anything else. One tip: Avoid underwire bras. They can be uncomfortable and may compress newly active milk ducts.

In your last month of pregnancy, shop for nursing bras if you're planning to breastfeed. These differ from regular maternity

What Size Are You?

Not everyone has access to a shop with trained bra-fitters. If you don't, take a few minutes to figure out your bra size on your own. Chances are, it has changed from your pre-pregnancy size. Use the size you come up with here as a starting place—every manufacturer's bras are a little different.

First, measure across your chest and back, just under your arms, rounding up to the next even number as necessary. This is your band size. Next, measure your chest again, this time at the fullest part of your breasts. Subtract the first measurement you took (the one under your arms) from the second measurement and use the chart below to find your cup size:

Result	Cup Size
2 to 2½"	B
2½ to 3½"	C
3½ to 4½"	D
4½ to 5"	E
5 to 6"	F
6 to 7"	G

bras in that they have cups that can be unhooked for easy access. Again, have a professional fitting and spend what's necessary to get the support and comfort you need. And buy several. Even if you use absorbent nursing pads, your nursing bras will get wet fairly often—and wearing a damp bra is a good way to contract a breast infection.

Most women prefer not to buy nursing bras for general use during pregnancy; the opening-cup feature that makes these great for nursing does mean that they don't lie as smoothly under clothing as a regular maternity bra will. In addition (amazing as it may seem), your cup size may well be larger while you're nursing than it is during pregnancy.

Ease your back with a maternity belt. Perhaps the least understood but most useful piece of underwear for your third trimester is a maternity belt. No, not the kind that holds up your pants. Developed by an orthopedic engineer, this is a simple but ingenious contraption of strong, comfortable elastic (often covered with soft fabric) that fits around your lower back and under your belly to cradle the often uncomfortable baby weight that can cause back strain, abdominal discomfort, or sciatic pain toward the end of your pregnancy. Originally designed to be worn discretely under your clothing, some maternity wear makers offer maternity belts in bold colors and bright patterns. Wear them on the outside, particularly over a leotard or yoga clothing, to provide support during exercise. These are widely available from maternity stores and catalogs.

PAMPER YOUR FEET

In her 8th month of pregnancy, first-grade teacher Meghan, 26, and her students hosted an art day. As parents arrived at the classroom, Meghan greeted them wearing her most beautiful maternity dress, a stylish batik scarf, and rhinestone bedecked flip-flops. When one of the moms commented on her fancy footwear, a 6-year-old student was quick to interject, "Hey, she usually goes barefoot!" Meghan sheepishly admitted that her feet were so swollen she kicked off her shoes as soon as she entered the classroom each morning. Unfortunately, most of us can't walk around at work barefoot, much as we'd like to. And pregnancy can wreak havoc on your feet. Swelling, itching, and aching are more common than not, and you may find that your feet increase at least a shoe size, rendering most of your footwear temporarily obsolete.

But unless you work as a hammock tester, there's probably no way to avoid these problems. There are ways to cope with them, however, first and foremost by having the right foot and leg wear. Just as you did when you went bra shopping, pay a visit to a reputable shoe store with a staff that knows as much about fitting shoes as about the latest shoe styles. Then follow these tips for 9 months of comfort:

✳ Shop for shoes in the afternoon. By then, your feet will be swollen and at their biggest.

✳ Give up the high heels, Cuban heels, and platforms early on. Your sense of balance changes as your weight shifts forward, so it's safer not to walk around on designer stilts. Look for elegant flats or shoes with low heels instead.

✳ Shop for a shoe that provides comfort; adjustability (with laces or straps) is a plus. If your workplace is sneaker-friendly, be grateful.

✳ Take the time to find something you like. It may be a while before your feet return to their pre-pregnancy Cinderella proportions.

✳ If your legs swell or you have a history of varicose veins, wear support stockings. Put them on first thing in the morning, even before you get out of bed, to prevent swelling.

THE BODY BEAUTIFUL

When you get dressed for work, you don't just put on your clothes and dash out the door. No matter what your job is, you spend some time fixing your hair and applying makeup. These steps are as much a part of getting dressed as selecting the right dress or slacks. So you should know that pregnancy brings changes in your hair and skin as well as in the shape of your body. You'll need to give these areas of your body as much attention as your clothing to maintain your professional image at work.

THAT PREGNANT GLOW

Changes in your skin may be one of the first pregnancy-related changes you notice. Either you'll begin glowing like a healthy rose, or have complexion problems to rival those of any troubled teen. In both cases, the cause is the same—hormone fluctuations.

If you're lucky enough to be granted a model's skin during this period, make the most of it. Lighten up on your makeup, accent what you have with minimal (but good-quality) mascara and lipstick, and omit what you don't need.

If you're faced with the opposite problem—acne the likes of which you haven't seen since you were 16—bring up the topic at your next doctor's visit. Many over-the-counter acne treatments contain ingredients that should be avoided during pregnancy. Consult your doctor about any you are now using, or to see if you need a new product.

Pre-existing skin conditions may also get worse during pregnancy. That doesn't mean you can use your pre-pregnancy medications, though. Prescription skin medications may not be safe for your baby; check with your doctor about any medication you've been using. And don't think you're in the clear if your prescription medication is topical, rather than oral. Even though you put them

147

on your skin, topical medications can be absorbed through your skin and enter your bloodstream, then cross the placental barrier into your baby.

Some doctors recommend you avoid acne-fighting and exfoliating skin care products containing the following chemicals, especially during your first trimester:

* Benzoyl peroxide
* Salicylic acid
* Glycolic acid
* Hydroxy acids
* Tretinoin, vitamin A (sold as Retin-A, Altinac, Avita, Renova, and Micro Gel)
* Tetracycline
* Botulinum toxin (marketed as Botox)

Basic skin care is the best way to retain the pregnant glow and avoid problems. Cleanse twice a day with a mild soap or cleanser appropriate to your skin type, and use the most gentle facial products possible. Try toning products such as witch hazel, and natural scrubs like pastes made with oatmeal, ground almonds, or salt. Moisturize as needed, again, selecting a product appropriate for your skin type; many pregnant women find their skin dry and itchy. Sunscreen is also more important than it's ever been. Unprotected skin can develop dark or brownish spots or patches called melasma, also known as the "mask of pregnancy." Most of these dark patches disappear after your baby is born; in the meantime, a little artistry with a good foundation can even out these minor variations in skin tone.

African American and Hispanic women have their own set of pregnancy skin issues. While dark-skinned women are subject to melasma, their skin may also become ashy and blotchy during preg-

More Than Skin Deep

Some skin conditions that can change your skin's appearance during pregnancy go beyond the typical acne or dryness. Consult your doctor if you are concerned about any of the following, or if anything appears on your skin that you can't identify.

Rosacea. If you have rosacea, you'll have tell-tale red patches or blotches on your face and/or neck that appear or intensify with blushing or other circumstances associated with flushing. With severe rosacea, your nose may appear swollen. Rosacea is considered both a skin disorder and a vascular condition. Medical treatment is available, but several of the relevant medications have not been approved for use by women who are pregnant or nursing. To reduce symptoms naturally, avoid eating spicy foods, minimize your midday sun exposure, and allow hot beverages to cool a bit before drinking them. Consult your doctor about additional steps you can take to reduce your symptoms while pregnant.

Pityriasis rosea. Pityriasis appears as teardrop-shaped lesions, which typically begin on the trunk of the body and may spread from there. Although scaly and itchy, this condition typically disappears after pregnancy. In the meantime, ask your doctor whether the itching can be treated with cortisone cream or another product intended for treatment of poison ivy.

Pruritic urticarial papules (PUPP). Also known as Plaques of Pregnancy, PUPP is a relatively rare hormone-related condition that may occur during the third trimester of pregnancy. It's characterized by small bumps and itchy hives on the torso. Treatment with hydrating cream can relieve the itching. If you exhibit such symptoms, check with your doctor about the safest treatments.

Stretch marks. Red or silvery streaks that may appear on breasts, belly, thighs, or other expanding parts of your pregnant body. Whether you get stretch marks has more to do with genetics than anything else. Skin creams and ointments which promise to prevent or remove stretch marks may make skin feel good and relieve itching if skin is dry, but will likely do little to erase or minimize these lines. Sun exposure may make them appear more prominent, giving pregnant women another good reason to use sunscreen or sunblock.

nancy. Again, sunscreen is a must. Use it every day, even if the only sun exposure you expect is what you get walking from the parking lot at work into your building.

Finally, you may find that your lips are more prone to dryness during pregnancy. Make liberal use of petroleum jelly, lip balms, and moisturizing lipsticks.

The good news is that most pregnancy-related skin conditions are at their worst during the first trimester, and disappear completely once the baby is born and your hormones return to normal.

HAIR TODAY, GONE TOMORROW

Finally, a part of your body that pregnancy tends to enhance. During pregnancy, regular hair loss slows dramatically, leaving most pregnant women with lush, thicker tresses. The bad news: Expect to lose a lot of it soon after your baby is born. Don't panic when you start finding your brush filled with hair; you aren't going bald, just getting back to normal (we normally lose some hair every day).

Because pregnancy brings changes in your hair, this isn't a great time for a drastic new cut. It's a good idea, however, to keep your hair neatly trimmed and find a low-maintenance hair-care routine.

And stick to your natural color and texture. While the jury is still out on the use of permanent hair color and hair bleaching during pregnancy, it's best to err on the side of caution. Most products for the temporary or semi-permanent coloring of hair have been determined to be safe for pregnant women. Again, check with your doctor as well as your stylist. If you do decide to color your hair, keep in mind that the hormonal changes of pregnancy may affect the way your hair takes color, particularly if you color your hair at home. Your tried-and-true favorite color may suddenly look less like "caramel mousse" and more like "brassy broad." If you're already working with a professional to color your hair, make sure he or she knows you're pregnant.

In general, try to avoid harsh chemicals or treatments that can overheat you—set that hair dryer on cool. As for permanents or hair straighteners, the experts haven't reached a definitive decision. Some doctors believe that anything that involves strong, bad-smelling chemicals is probably not good for your baby. In any case, pregnancy may also make a permanent or straightener less effective.

Pregnancy affects your body profoundly, but there's no reason why you can't go on feeling—and looking—like yourself during these months. No matter where you work and what your style, you should be able to maintain a look that works for you and for your job. Keep comfort, functionality, and above all, safety issues paramount for you and your baby, and the two of you will sail through your pregnancy in high style.

Maintaining Strong Nails

Nails, like skin, may end up looking healthy and terrific during your pregnancy, or they may become dull, dry, and brittle. How they look doesn't seem to be related to anything dietary or to the use of prenatal vitamins—mostly, the way your pregnancy affects your nails (and skin) is largely the luck of the draw.

There's no known danger associated with nail polishes or removers (though it is advisable to use as few chemical products as possible during pregnancy). If you have professional manicures or pedicures (a boon for when you can't reach your own feet any more), make sure that the salon is licensed and that it follows good hygiene to prevent infection and the spread of fungi. Consider bringing your own pedicure or manicure kit if you're not sure. Or, better yet, talk your partner into a foot massage and pedicure/manicure.

KEYS TO KEEPING THE BALANCE

X Maternity wear is more varied than it's ever been. Look for clothes that make you feel like *you*, and choose them according to their suitability for your workplace's unique style, just as you chose your pre-pregnancy clothes.

X Most women start wearing maternity clothes in their 4th month, but this varies; women who are carrying multiples or who have already had a baby will need maternity wear sooner.

X Economize by borrowing maternity clothes from friends and relatives. Don't overlook consignment shops, thrift stores, and discount stores.

X Buy the most comfortable and supportive undergarments you can afford, and have your bras professionally fitted, if possible.

X Hair, skin, and nails will either shine with incredible beauty and vigor during pregnancy, or will give you no end of trouble. Choose beauty products with the baby's safety in mind.

8

BREAKING AWAY: PLANNING YOUR LEAVE

didn't do all the planning for my leave that, in retrospect, I wish I had," says Shellie, 32, a grant review administrator for a federal agency. "My boss didn't hire anyone to replace me temporarily, and most of my tasks were tossed to other folks at work who weren't prepared for them. As a result, I was on the phone all the time, fielding calls from the office about where this file or these presentation materials were, or about the status of this grant application. Several times I had to go in for whole days at a time, weeks before I'd intended to go back to work." Don't be like Shellie. The more carefully you plan your family leave, the more fruitful the leave will be—and it will be easier to make a reasonably smooth transition back to the office when it ends.

Months before your leave begins, consider the tasks you'll need to accomplish in order to have a true maternity leave, one without daily calls or e-mails from the office. It won't be easy; more than half the women who take family leave report that they get called by the office, sometimes often. Of course there will be times and circumstances under which you want to remain in touch with work, but these should be arranged at your convenience—when the baby is napping, for instance, or after she's asleep for the night. If you constantly have to put out fires by telephone or e-mail, then you aren't really away from work. So read on to learn how you can plan a leave that results in minimal intrusion from the office.

DIFFERENT STROKES

The amount and type of planning you need to do for a smooth family leave depends on several things. The first, of course, is the type of work you do. If any of the following describes your job, your planning will be more complex. If all of them do, get started as soon as you possibly can.

* You are high up on the management ladder, supervising several employees. Your actual title matters less than the way your office hierarchy is structured: The more people who report to you, the more detailed your planning needs to be.

* You have a great degree of variability in your job from day to day. For instance, Cathy, 29, is a public health nurse in a rural area who regularly visits three health clinics a week, coordinates health care efforts with the nurses at several schools, and teaches weekly first aid and CPR classes. In addition, she spends time juggling administrative tasks related to finding and maintaining funding for health care projects in her area. No two work days are ever the same for her, and she needs to coordinate her work with clinic and school administrators and local authorities responsible for funding. Shannon, 32, is also a nurse, but she keeps regular hours at a small suburban pediatric clinic, and her day-to-day duties are pretty much the same. Making sure all of her job responsibilities are met will be more difficult for Cathy, whose daily activities are more varied and involve more people in different offices.

* You generally determine your own agenda during the work day or work week, working with minimal supervision. Mathea, 36, an architect who started her own firm 2 years ago, makes all her own decisions regarding her agenda, and plans her to-do list according to what jobs are pending. A colleague has offered to supervise her on-going projects and the few assistants on her staff during the time Mathea wants to take off after her baby is born. But because Mathea determines what needs to be done each day on the basis of how projects are progressing and what problems need to be addressed, it will be difficult to provide specific instructions to her colleague. Mathea realizes that she will have to continue to be closely involved in how things are going at the office while she's on leave.

* Your responsibilities require a great deal of interaction with numerous coworkers on the job. Sylvia, 26, is a cashier at a large chain bookstore. She interacts with customers all day long, but when she goes on maternity leave in 2 months, her responsibilities can be handled fairly easily by other cashiers who do essentially what she does every day. Deborah, 27, is a manager at the same store, who will be having her baby at about the same time. Because Deborah's job involves regular interactions with cashiers, stock clerks, café workers, upper level management, and other employees, she will need to do more planning to make sure that each of these areas will run smoothly while she's away.

* You are responsible for meeting the needs of specific clients or maintaining mutually beneficial relationships with vendors. Your planning needs to include specific arrangements for ensuring that someone assumes these responsibilities in your absence.

No matter what your position, the more thought you put into planning your leave, the more everyone benefits. Your boss will be able to relax, knowing someone is covering your tasks; your clients

His and Hers

If your husband is also planning to take leave under FMLA, he needs to follow much of the advice throughout this chapter and this book. Make sure he also gives 30 days notice to his employer. Remember, if you both work for companies covered under FMLA, you may take up to 12 weeks of job protected leave *each*. If, however, you and your husband work for the same company, your employer can limit your leave time to a *total* of 12 weeks between you, rather than 12 weeks *each*. The FMLA regulations specify that fathers, as well as mothers, are eligible for leave under the law. Although it refers to "husbands and wives," it does allow for coverage of partners in common-law marriages to the extent recognized by law in many states. Check with your human resources department for clarification on how this applies in your state.

Additionally, both of you should coordinate your respective leaves. Since you're the one doing the physical labor, you will most likely want to take most or all of your leave immediately after the baby's birth. This not only gives you precious time to bond with your new one, but also to recover physically from the pregnancy and delivery, and to get a good start on breastfeeding. Many dads take a week or two off immediately after the birth, then distribute the remaining time in a way that works for both—or all three—of you.

For instance, you may want your partner's leave to begin when yours ends, delaying the time until you need child care. Or you may want to alternate, both of you working part-time for a while on opposite days. Alternatively, one or both of you may want to save some time for those inevitable days when the baby is too ill for child care. Think of the FMLA as your allowance and the available days off as penny candy—plan in advance to decide how you'll spend it to get the most for your money.

won't even notice you're missing, because they will receive uninterrupted service that meets the standards you've taught them to expect; and you'll have a more relaxing leave because you won't spend your leave fretting over whether—and how—things are being handled. Your re-entry will be smoother as well, because you did the important, up-front planning.

10 STEPS FOR PLANNING YOUR LEAVE

Sometimes, it seems the folks at work can't get along without us for just a day. So it can seem overwhelming to plan a leave of a number of weeks or months. It helps to break down the task into 10 small steps. Follow each carefully, and by the time those first labor pains hit, you should be as relaxed as a yoga instructor (about leaving work, at least).

Step 1: Set a (tentative) date. Begin by trying to pinpoint when you'll be going on leave. Of course, babies hate to be pinpointed. Breathes there a child who arrived in this world on its due date? Oh, okay, maybe one or two, but even if you're planning to work right up until your water breaks, try to build a little flexibility into your schedule.

Step 2: Create your "I'm-gonna-be-a-momma" to-do list. Get a sheet of paper and draw a line vertically down the middle. At the top of the left side, write "Work Commitments." At the top of the right, write "Personal and Family Events." Down the left margin, list each month of pregnancy beginning with the third or fourth month—earlier than this, there isn't much to do except take your vitamins, attend any scheduled prenatal appointments, and enjoy being pregnant. Now complete the chart as best you can, filling in events and chores associated with each time period in each of the two worlds in which you're now living. On the work side, include ongoing projects, conferences, performance reviews, and vacations (don't take too much vacation time, though, if you're going to be needing vacation pay as income during your leave). On the home side, include important dates such as your amniocentesis screening and any other prenatal tests, your mom's birthday, your plan to investigate child care options, the family reunion. Here's a sample:

Month	*Work Commitments*	*Personal and Family Commitments*
Fourth	Double-check with human resources re: leave policies Sketch out ideal leave plan Make appointment to tell boss about pregnancy	Amnio—5/4 2:00 Visit day care centers Call nanny referral gal
Fifth	Check calendar from now until get-away date and decide which events can be cleared, postponed, or reassigned	Investigate childbirth preparedness classes and register in advance
Sixth	Regional sales conference Arrange and conduct performance reviews	Confirm health insurance coverage
Seventh	Create plan for delegating work while on leave Create plan for staying in touch	Call pediatricians, make appointments Dad's birthday Our anniversary
Eighth	Touch base with clients and vendors Clean desk	Make and freeze soups, casseroles, etc. Choose birth announcements Baby shower (look surprised)
Ninth	Computer housekeeping Keep coworkers up to date on work issues	Plan route to hospital from home and from office; pack bag

Step 3: Plan for your return. I know it seems like it's far in the future, but any planning for your leave must also include a plan for your return. I'll tell you more about how to insure a smooth re-entry in chapter 10. Here is where you lay the groundwork for that easy return.

From the beginning, discussions of your upcoming leave should be somewhat vague about when it will end. Your employer is legally entitled to ask you to touch base at reasonable intervals, and he may also inquire about how long you intend to stay out, as long as this is not done in a discriminatory way. For instance, "You mothers always stay out longer than you need to" is definitely inappropriate. So on your end, just say, "I will most likely be out for 8 weeks," not, "I will be back on June 2." Many things can happen during a family leave to change your plans and make you want to stay out longer—or, surprisingly—to come back early.

Also keep in mind that the Family Medical Leave Act (FMLA) permits employees to take less than the 12-week full-time leave offered, followed by a part-time period as you phase back to work. This kind of arrangement provides partial income while allowing you to extend your leave, and may be more conducive to continued breastfeeding as you return to work. Plus, your employer may be pleased to have you back earlier (even part time) than if you took the entire FMLA leave all at once. Such a plan may also provide a good compromise for you and your employer if you are not eligible to take leave under FMLA.

Step 4: Get organized. If you weren't a terribly organized person before your pregnancy, now is the time to change. Even if you think you've already got your job pretty well ordered, consider how someone else might view it. Sure, *you* know precisely where a certain document is—in the middle of that 6-inch-high pile of papers on the floor—but will a coworker be able to find it? *You* have a brilliant system for categorizing files on your computer, but would it take the consulting services of a clairvoyant with a crystal ball for anyone else to divine how it works?

Make the transition as seamless as possible by leaving a tidy workspace for those who will fill in for you in your absence.

* Clean your desk. Mine through those stacks of papers and file (or toss) them appropriately.
* Make sure your address list—virtual or electronic—is up to date.
* Take home any personal items that are valuable or irreplaceable.
* Clean the vertical surfaces, too. Clear off bulletin boards or white boards, leaving only materials that will be useful to your staff or replacement.

Step 5: Catch up and work ahead. If you will be turning much of your job over to coworkers who will have to take on your duties while completing their own, be merciful. Don't leave them with a full slate of tasks you should have completed before you went into labor. Use the months leading up to your delivery to finish projects and tie up loose ends, or at least arrange matters so someone just starting to fill your shoes will be able to understand the tasks at hand and resume them relatively seamlessly. This is not the time to start some major new project, if you can help it. If not, consider bringing in a coworker from the beginning to minimize confusion when you depart.

And regardless of when you're due, plan as if you were going out tomorrow, especially once you pass your 7th month. Anything can happen. Then, if you deliver early or are put on bed rest for the last weeks or months of your pregnancy, you (and your coworkers) won't be caught completely unaware. For instance, Peggy, a 28-year-old junior high school teacher, was a week away from her due date and, she thought, a week away from her maternity leave. But when she was showing her substitute, Dianne, around the science wing of the school, she suddenly stopped walking and laughed nervously. "Can you start tomorrow instead of next week?" she asked. "My water just broke."

Step 6: Write it all down. If yours is a job in which the tasks of one day are very much like the tasks on all days, a short list of instructions should suffice. But if your work responsibilities are complex and varied, leave yourself enough time to create an instruction

Working on Bed Rest: Don't Even Think About It

One in five pregnant women is put on partial or complete bed rest at some point during her pregnancy, usually to delay the onset of labor for as long as possible to prevent the often life-threatening complications common in premature infants. You may be put on bed rest if you have premature labor, threatened miscarriage, an incompetent cervix, placenta previa, pre-eclampsia, or any number of other conditions in which premature delivery is possible. You may also be put on bed rest if you are carrying multiples, especially more than two babies.

Being put on bed rest is a serious approach to a severe problem, and is not to be taken lightly. Your healthcare provider may recommend you lie down (usually on your left side) for most of the day, allowing you to get up to shower, go to the bathroom, or prepare a quick meal. Or she may insist on complete bed rest (including the use of a bedpan). She may also order one or more medications to prevent contractions and encourage fetal lung development. This is an important part of taking care of your baby, but these are heavy-duty drugs and will likely make you feel peculiar—weak, shaky, and fuzzy-headed.

If you're ordered to bed, the stress of worrying about the work that's going undone while you lie there can make a bad situation worse. So *don't.* No project, no deadline, no job is important enough to jeopardize your welfare and that of your baby. Stay in bed, rent every movie you've ever wanted to see, read every book, write a journal to your baby, *relax.* Allow others to wait on you for a change, bring you food, give you sponge baths, play games with you. But let the office take care of itself—every day you make it without going into labor is a gift you're giving your baby.

"To Whom It May Concern . . ."

You can use the following sample letter as a template for writing your own letter to your staff and co-workers about how your work responsibilities should be handled during your leave.

June 18, 2004

To my staff and co-workers:

I anticipate being out on leave full time from the end of June through early September. When I return, I'll be working part-time until resuming a full-time work schedule in October. In the meantime, I have made arrangements to stay in contact with the office through regular e-mail and weekly phone contacts with my assistant, Cheryl Smith, and my supervisor, Alice Brown. I would be very grateful if most contacts could be made through Cheryl, particularly during the earliest part of my leave. I am, of course, always available at a.jones@widgets.com.

Ongoing projects

While I'm away the following office staff will serve as the point people for these accounts:

Allied Whatsis	*Tom, Cindy*
Widgets Today	*Elizabeth*
Widget World	*Al*
Diversity committee	*Sherri*

I've left all relevant materials for each account with the people listed; these can also be accessed on my computer:

manual for your job, along with clear information about your responsibilities and the chain of command.

Ideally, you will turn this information into a handbook, a sort of "My Job and Welcome To It" approach. (See "To Whom It May Concern . . ." above for a template.) You can put this in a loose-leaf notebook, in transferable PDA files, or simply in photocopied pages bound in a report cover. Such a handbook should contain the following, as well as anything else that pertains to your particular job:

Account	File Name	Password
Allied Whatsis	c: allwhat	newbaby
Widgets Today	c: widgtd	newbaby
Widget World	c:widworld	newbaby
Diversity committee	c:diversco	office1

The remaining pages of this folder contain information which I hope will help you to take care of any tasks that arise while I'm gone. I've included:

* *My home phone and fax numbers and e-mail addresses. If you need to overnight anything to me, Cheryl can take care of it for you.*

* *Progress reports, in a separate section for each client, containing a recent history of all contacts and the current status of each account, along with specific notes for handling each one.*

* *Contact info (including billing) for each client.*

If anything else should arise, Cheryl can help you. In a real emergency, of course, I can always be reached at home.

Thanks,
Angela

P.S. Thank you all again for the wonderful shower and the fabulous baby carriage—I know I'll get tons of use out of it!

* Contact information for you. Phone, cell phone, fax, e-mail, home address in case your office needs to use overnight mail or messenger something to you.

* A list of all ongoing projects. Limit each project to one page. On each page, include the names of staff members working on the project, a description of the project and brief update on its progress, all interim and final due dates, names and contact information for anyone working off-site or from another company (including consultants).

✳ A list of all direct reports and contact information. Also include a list of anyone who will be handling your job while you're out, and their specific responsibilities as well as their contact information (phone, fax, e-mail).

✳ A master list of file names and file locations—both virtual and paper—relevant to each project.

✳ Procedural notes for any activities for which you're regularly responsible: opening the shop in the morning, setting the security alarm as you leave at night, feeding the cat who hangs out in the studio.

Be specific. For instance, if you work retail, your manual should include not only notes about venders, customers, regular deliveries, security, and banking, but also the fact that you have to jiggle the key in the upper lock to the back door before it will open.

Clearly, not every job will lend itself to this approach, but a surprising number will. If you're a teacher, you're probably already accustomed to having lesson plans available for a substitute. In addition to your normal lesson plans, add details about the students' usual schedule (for example, remind the class to wear sneakers for gym on Mondays and Wednesdays); special needs (Miranda and Luke are lactose intolerant and need to see the nurse before snack time to get their medication); or custody warnings (Sue Ellen should not be released to anyone but her mother).

Step 7: Meet with those taking over your projects. Discuss any concerns you—or they—might have about specific projects or responsibility. Because babies can arrive at unpredictable times, do this at least by the end of your 8th month. You can then have shorter weekly meetings as needed during your remaining pre-baby time to keep things nicely up to date.

During these meetings, designate someone as a contact person for you during your leave, and request that all communication be routed through him or her. Make sure this person knows to screen these communications carefully and to call you only when it is a true emergency. Also specify that the first 2 to 3 weeks of your leave is a "no call, no e-mail zone," during which you should be contacted only in the event of the most dire circumstances. After that, make yourself more accessible, within limits. For instance, you might want to set a regular time to touch base—say, every Thursday during the baby's nap time. This way, miscellaneous issues can be handled in one weekly call instead of six. When you do check in with work, make sure you get not only a business briefing, but also an environmental briefing—a sense of how people feel about your absence. Complaints from coworkers that they are being unduly inconvenienced by your leave should be addressed as soon as possible, whether they are justified or not. (More about this in chapter 10.)

This is a best-of-all-possible-worlds scenario, of course, and in real life things rarely go as planned. Your replacement may quit, leaving the office begging you to come in "just for a few days." You're going to have to use your best judgment about requests like these, but do consider saying no. Make sure all other avenues have been exhausted before making yourself, in essence, the sub for your sub.

Step 8: Give a tour. Plan this for fairly late in your pregnancy. Give the person, or people, who will be filling in for you a "tour" of your job, whether that's a physical tour of the shop you manage, the classroom in which you teach, or the factory floor you oversee, or a more contained tour of your desk and computer. It may even be a "tour" of your clients. For instance, if you're a healthcare provider, such as a psychiatrist or a social worker, you'll most likely refer your clients to another practitioner who will take over for you in your absence. Set aside time to discuss your patients with your substitute.

Step 9: Manage your e-mail. At least a week before your due date, unsubscribe or switch to "no-mail" status on any e-mail listserves you're subscribed to, or reroute them to your home computer. Create an automatic response program for incoming e-mails you receive that alerts the sender that you're on leave and directs them to the person covering for you.

If you don't have a secretary or assistant at work, ask a coworker to sort your snail mail for you several times a week, showing her which should be junked, which should be passed on to those covering for you, which can wait for your return, and which you'd like to have delivered to your home, like personal mail or professional journals.

Step 10: Clean your virtual desk. Plan to leave a tidy computer behind you, particularly if supervisors and coworkers will have access to it while you're on leave. Remove any personal files and even remotely inappropriate documents. Make sure any files your coworkers will need during your absence are easy to access and understand. For instance, flesh out any sketchy notes to yourself to make them intelligible to others, and neaten them up. If there are things on your computer you don't want others seeing, such as your annual evaluation, protect the files with passwords (but make sure you write down the password somewhere so you can access them upon your return).

Reorganize your computer (and desk) files as necessary. Establish folders for specific projects, or by client, month, quarter—whatever makes the most sense for your workplace. Create a master list detailing how your files are organized and place a hard copy of this master list in the handbook you're creating.

Make copies of important folders and files; back up copies for the workplace on floppies or CD-RW, and make an extra copy you can take home if you need to access it while you're out (unless you can access your office computer remotely from home). Archive files no longer in use by putting them on a CD-RW, floppy, or zip disk.

Pass on your passwords. If you use a personal password to gain access to files on your computer, you might not want to share that one

Braxton Hicks Contractions: Practice Makes Perfect

So you're standing at the copy machine when you feel a small but unmistakable cramp in your abdomen. Is it time to put your escape-to-the-hospital plan into action? Maybe. But before you bow out, make sure you aren't just having Braxton Hicks contractions.

Braxton Hicks are your body's way of practicing for labor. Many women mistake these for the real deal, however, especially in late pregnancy. But Braxton Hicks can generally be distinguished from true labor pains. Genuine labor pains tend to be more painful than Braxton Hicks, so painful that it's difficult to carry on a conversation during the contraction. Real labor pains are usually regular, becoming more frequent as labor progresses, while Braxton Hicks contractions are intermittent and generally end after a brief period. If you're not sure whether your pains are really labor, try changing positions or taking a short walk. If the pains increase or become more regular or frequent, it's time to call your doctor or midwife; if they subside, it was probably just another rehearsal.

As you near your intended date of departure, make sure you know the quickest route from your office to the hospital, and arrange in advance for a friend at work to drive you there in case you need to leave quickly. Do *not* try to drive yourself to the hospital while you're in labor.

---

with the whole office. For items that need to be seen and worked on by your coworkers, create new passwords as needed.

KEEP THE MOTOR RUNNING

The key to making a clean get-away from the office as you begin your family leave is to be prepared. Make sure your coworkers know how your absence may affect them, and keep ugly surprises to a minimum by giving them the access and information they need to fill in for you successfully while you're away. Strike a reasonable balance between asking for privacy and being available, and you'll not only streamline your departure but also make it easier and more pleasant to return after your baby is born.

KEYS TO KEEPING
THE BALANCE

Transitioning back to work following your family leave will go more smoothly if you've paved the way by handling your leave-taking in an organized manner, making life easier for those who will be filling in for you.

If you and your spouse both plan to take leave under FMLA, make sure you both declare your intent at least 30 days prior to the date you want your leave to begin. Work together to coordinate your available weeks off to maximize the time you can be with your new baby and with each other, thus delaying the use of day care.

Make sure your supervisors, those who report to you, and those who will be covering or filling in for you understand their responsibilities and have access to all the materials they will need. Don't forget to touch base as needed with outside vendors, consultants, and clients.

Designate a contact person at your office and try to have all office communications go through her at regularly scheduled times to give you and your family as much privacy and rest as possible.

One pregnant woman in five ends up on bed rest at some point. If it happens to you, don't try to work at home during this time. Your health and your baby's health must be your only priorities now.

9

THE CHALLENGE
OF CHILD CARE

S omething unnerving happens as soon as you find out you're
pregnant. You start to hear child care stories—*terrible* child
care stories. The one about the caregiver who absconded with
her young charge. The one about the nanny who was so busy talking
to her friends in the park that she didn't notice when the baby
crawled away. The one about the babysitter who left the baby in the
hot car, or the daycare provider who shook the baby, or—*enough*!
Suffice it to say that you're going to hear stories that confirm your
worst nightmares about child care. The sad truth is that such things
do happen, but the good news is that there are plenty of wonderful
day care settings out there.

Day care is a fact of life for more than half of all infants in the
United States. Yet years of lobbying by child advocates have failed
to convince the federal government to assume any responsibility for
this care. In the absence of uniform and appropriate nationwide
standards for child care in this country, you, as a parent, are your
child's best, and often only, advocate. If you're a new parent, this
can be a daunting task.

The sad fact is that the child care system in the United States isn't much of a system at all. Most care is unregulated, good care-givers are hard to find, and high-quality care—especially for in-fants—is expensive. A long-term study of child care in the United States, conducted in the 1990s and published in 1998, was carried out under the auspices of the National Institutes of Child Health and Development. Ten universities around the country gathered data on 1,300 children and their child care facilities. Nearly half of all of the day care settings studied were found to be of substandard quality when measured against generally acceptable standards for caregiver training, staff-to-child ratios, and age-appropriate programming.

None of this provides much comfort to a mom looking for the perfect caregiver: a mix of Mary Poppins, Mr. Rogers, and Grandma.

FINDING MARY POPPINS

All is not doom and despair, however. There are wonderful, work-able care arrangements available for parents who know what to look for, and who are committed to putting as much (if not more) effort into finding and maintaining great child care as they put into their jobs. A measure of luck doesn't hurt, either, as Ann, a 31-year-old journalist who often covers parenting topics, learned.

Ann sometimes thinks the Child Care Fairy must have tapped her with a tiny but powerful wand. "We had searched and searched for a good day care arrangement, but it was sheer luck that led us to our son's great caregiver," she says. "My husband and I bought our first house the same week our baby was born. It turned out that our new neighbor had a 6-month-old son and was looking for someone to help make her child care arrangement work. Her husband's sec-retary's sister—got all that?—wanted to provide infant care in her home so she could be there for her *own* toddler son. But she wanted to care for only one baby, and she wanted that baby full time. Because my neighbor worked 3 days a week, and I needed only part-time care and had a flexible schedule, we were able to share the secretary's sister. The caregiver took my neighbor's son on Mondays and Wednesdays, mine on Tuesdays and Thursdays, and we coaxed her into taking both boys on Fridays. Not only did we get good, loving care, but the caregiver got a full-time income, and the two boys grew up as friends right from the beginning."

Although Ann attributes such a satisfying care giving arrangement to luck, she sells herself a bit short when she makes this claim. No matter how fortuitous it was that she met the right people at the right time, she and her husband did their homework and knew what to look for in a care setting.

THE CHILD CARE SYSTEM THAT ISN'T

The vast majority of what's sometimes called "other-than-mother" care in the United States is a mishmash of arrangements. Many families have to cobble together a patchwork of arrangements throughout their child's different stages of development, in addition to handling their own work schedule. In other words, it can take not

The New Child Care Research

Child care research tells us one important thing about positive outcomes. Mothers who feel fulfilled and stimulated by their jobs, and those who leave their jobs and stay at home because they find this a more rewarding way of life, have children who tend to be happily and securely attached—kids who grow and develop well. But working moms who dislike or resent working, or stay-at-home moms who feel stymied and trapped in this role, are more likely to have insecure and unhappy children. The moral: If mama ain't happy, ain't nobody happy.

just research, money, planning, and luck to arrive at a satisfactory child care plan—but also a lot of creativity.

Take Miranda, 38, a middle school principal. She not only works a regular 8:30 A.M. to 5:00 P.M. day, but often has to stay late at school for PTA meetings, to attend evening sessions of the Board of Education, or to meet with parents who are unavailable during the weekday. Her husband, Frank, is a police officer who works changing shifts. He might work nights for a few months, then days, but must also be available at short notice for emergencies in the small Tennessee town where they live.

Their 7-month-old baby, Tasha, has it made during the summers, when Miranda works only 3 weeks, and stays at home with her during the remaining school vacation weeks. During the school year, Tasha goes to a family day care provider in the mornings, but must be picked up by mid-afternoon, when the caregiver's own children return from school. If Frank is on the day shift, his mom takes Tasha after the caregiver's day ends. If he's working nights, he cares for her until Miranda gets home. But if Miranda has a night meeting and Frank has to work the night shift, his 16-year-old niece comes to their home to stay with Tasha. Unless *she* has an evening school event or, as happens more and more often, a date. Then Miranda's mom takes the baby, but she will baby-sit only at her own house. If Miranda's meeting runs late, both Tasha and her grandmother will be asleep, and so Tasha spends the night at her grandmother's house. And if one or more of these players gets sick, or is otherwise unavailable, the whole arrangement can fall apart like the house of cards that it is.

Within this fragile framework, Tasha is always in the care of someone who loves her, but the sheer number of changes she might encounter in any given week is stressful for everyone, particularly for a baby. "You wouldn't think a baby experiences stress," says

Miranda, "but on a day when she's been with three different caregivers, she's just worn out and cranky, and then she sleeps badly and we're all exhausted the next day—when it starts again."

RULES AND REGULATIONS

Schools have them. Hospitals have them. Even dog kennels have them. But the day care center or family day care home you're checking out for your baby does not have them. What are they? Federal mandates regulating quality of care. Instead, we have 50 different sets of child care regulations, one for each state. You may be fortunate enough to live in a state that has appropriate rules for the safety and well-being of the children in child care. Or you may not, since state standards for child care range from stellar to woefully inadequate. The good ones guarantee your child a safe and developmentally appropriate environment. The not-so-good ones amount to little more than state-sanctioned child neglect.

In Idaho, for instance, a single caregiver can legally care for six infants at a time. Just imagine trying to provide basic custodial care to this many babies—safeguarding, feeding, and diapering—on your own, let alone having the time and resources to engage in warm, responsive interactions, or, in an emergency, to get them all out of a burning building. In Massachusetts, however, a single caregiver can watch only three infants.

Babies are babies are babies, no matter what part of the country they live in, and they all have the same needs for a safe environment and consistent, responsive, developmentally appropriate care. Until we have more uniform policies across the country, the responsibility rests with parents to create their own standards and find care facilities that meet them.

It's not that we don't know what those standards should be.

Child Care Standards 101

Research shows that children do better in daycare if the home or facility in which they are cared for adheres to certain standards in the following areas:

Caregiver/child ratios. Each worker should be responsible for the care of no more than three infants, four toddlers, or five preschoolers at once, and no more than six infants (with two caregivers) should be cared for at a time in any given child care home or center.

Continuity. Most child care workers are paid less than poverty-level wages (often with no benefits), so it's no wonder turnover is high. A study conducted by the Center for the Child Care Workforce found that from 1994 to 2000, 75 percent of the staff in child care centers left and were replaced. But children—infants in particular—need continuity in order to develop a sense that their world is a stable, predictable, manageable place in which they are loved and cared for. When checking out center care, ask the director what percentage of the staff leaves in a typical year, and how long, on average, staff members stay.

Caregiver training. In settings in which caregivers have appropriate child development training, there are more child-caregiver interactions and a greater amount of verbal stimulation, and abuse is far less likely to occur because caregivers have appropriate expectations of child behavior. Though there are few hard and fast standards for caregiver training, a good background might include at least 2 years of college or vocational school with an emphasis on child development or early childhood education.

Developmentally appropriate care. Does your child's care meet his developmental needs? The care and play needs of children in different groups require different activities and materials. Children of all ages need continuity of care and a safe environment, but look for the following as well:

Early childhood educators, developmental psychologists, and pediatricians have developed such standards based on years of research. But their recommendations (described in "Child Care Standards 101" above) are generally ignored.

Although all states require licenses for child care providers,

Infants need to be hugged, held, carried, sung to, and talked to. It is never too early to read to children, and even very young babies respond well to being shown picture books. As they progress to sitting on their own, creeping, and crawling, infants need baby-safe toys to finger, mouth, and bang together, and safe materials of different textures to feel. A baby's healthy desire to master her world will be exercised by giving her toys that safely open and close (books, boxes, drawers, and doors—always, of course, protecting little fingers), and toys that allow her to explore "in" and "out"—an unbreakable bowl of baby keys or links. In short, babies need a safe and well-supervised place to explore their environment.

Toddlers need opportunities to build on the above. Toys and safe materials for climbing and practicing new walking skills (push toys, sturdy wagons) are appropriate, as are soft cuddly toys to nurture, and make believe materials—toy phones and computers, dishes and play foods, brooms and toy lawn mowers for mimicking the adult world. Books can be slightly more complex as toddlers learn to identify pictures and sit still for very short stories. Toddlers also need materials to manipulate with their hands (simple puzzles, pounding benches, and so on), and ways to listen to and make music and begin to scribble and paint.

Preschoolers need an environment that's still safe, but more complex, and with reasonable structure. Preschoolers in a small group setting, for instance, should be learning to take turns, to play simple board or card games, and to sit still for a story or puppet show. Art and music activities can be more sophisticated (crayons are more often used for drawing than chewing on) and make-believe materials can be more complex, with dress-up toys and more elaborate settings for playing out fantasies. These need not be complicated or expensive—an empty cardboard box can function as an oven or a spaceship just as well as more realistic and pricey toy store versions.

much child care is unlicensed, occurring in private homes or in religious institutions that may not require licensing. Additionally, even in instances where licensing applies, few states have the time, money, or trained personnel to ensure that those providers comply with state regulations and standards. Still, research over the past decade from Yale University and other child development and social policy study centers indicates that, on average, licensed care provides a higher quality than unlicensed care.

Recent research conducted by the Families and Work Institute in New York City revealed that regulated day care is strongly associated with a warmer and more attentive child-caregiver relationship. Overall, studies find that good quality child care (in contrast to care of poorer quality) is associated with school readiness and better social skills, language development and stronger mother-child relationships, and lower incidence of behavior problems. Poor quality care is linked to a higher proportion of inappropriate behaviors as these children reach their toddler and preschool years, including poor impulse control and increased levels of aggression.

Part of the definition of quality has to do with caregiver training standards. Studies show that day care providers with some training in child development or early childhood education engage in more sensitive and appropriate caregiving that leads to improvements in children's cognitive and language development.

Overall, licensing of caregivers appears to promote higher-quality care. The reasons are varied, but one may be that people who take the time and spend the money to comply with state licensing requirements tend to be those who take what they're doing most seriously. Additionally, licensing can indicate a caregiver's commitment to her charges. Unfortunately, the Families and Work Institute study found that less than a third of mothers polled considered licensing of child care settings to be an important consideration in their choice of child care setting. This does not mean, of course, that quality of care isn't of tremendous concern to parents. When asked to name the things important to them in making child care choices, most parents name the very things upon which licensing is typically based. They want to know their child is safe, that their caregiver will keep them up to date about what's going on with their child, and that their caregiver will have a warm, attentive, and caring relationship with their child.

Too bad they can't get their child into Lee Ann's home-based daycare in a suburb of Boston. After working for very little pay in a reasonably safe but rather cheerless not-for-profit church day care center, Lee Ann, 45, decided she could do better for herself and for the children. She and her husband were lucky in that their property held two houses—they lived in one and rented the other. When their tenant's lease expired, they completely remodeled the house, turning it into a clean, modern, and child-friendly day care center.

There's a nap room with brand-new cribs for the babies, a quiet room for play and toddler naps on cots, a noisy room for building blocks and music, an art area, and a fenced back yard with safety-approved swings, sandbox, and picnic area.

Lee Ann hired another woman to work with her, and today the two care for two infants and three toddlers. "If the licensing officer had a concern or a suggestion, I did whatever she wanted to make it right," she says. "Most of my babies stay here until they're ready for preschool, and I've got a waiting list as long as your arm."

To be fair, an unlicensed daycare setting may not automatically mean it provides poor quality care. Consider the day care home where Liza, 30, an office manager for a large actuarial firm, takes her twin daughters. She loves the family day care provider there and once asked whether she'd ever considered applying for a state license. Turns out she had applied, but had been turned down after a home inspection. "She met all of their standards, except two: her home contained a spiral staircase and her family had a large Labrador retriever, both of which I knew about," says Liza. "While the girls were there, the dog was always in the basement with access to a spacious dog run in the back yard, and the spiral staircase that led to the second floor of her home was securely gated and inaccessible to my kids. It wasn't good enough for the state inspectors, but it was good enough for me. I just didn't see these things as presenting any risk to my daughters."

FINDING THE RIGHT CARE

In addition to the standards outlined in "Child Care Standards 101" (on page 174), there are other things you want to look for when choosing a care setting for your child:

✳ Does the caregiver smoke? Second-hand smoke has been linked to increased rates of respiratory illnesses such as bronchitis and asthma; the presence of matches or lighters and lit cigarettes also increases the potential for fire and burn hazards.

✳ If you plan to allow your caregiver to drive your child around, does she have a clean driving record, with no outstanding tickets, accidents, or other moving violations? Is her automobile insurance current and adequate? Does her car meet state inspections? Does she have an approved car seat for the baby?

✳ Does the facility have smoke detectors, fire extinguishers, and clearly marked and accessible emergency exits?

✳ Are the caregiver's immunizations up to date?

✳ Has the caregiver passed a police check?

✳ Is the facility appropriately child-safe? (I'll provide you with a list of specific things to check on page 194.)

✳ Does the facility permit spanking or other forms of corporal punishment? Make sure their discipline strategies match your own.

TYPES OF CARE

One of the first decisions you must make regarding child care is what type will best meet your needs and those of your child. Child care in the United States falls into three basic categories: in-home care, family day care, and center care. Each has its own advantages and disadvantages.

In-home care. In-home care, as the name implies, is provided within the child's own home, typically for only one child or for the children of only one family. According to the Children's Defense Fund, roughly 5 percent of children in care arrangements in the United States receive in-home care by a nanny or au pair, and it makes up the smallest category among the various child care settings. An additional 22 percent of children are cared for in their home by a relative. Arrangements of this kind are most likely to be used for children under age 2.

Although in-home care conjures up images of Mary Poppins and upper-income families, such care is more likely to be provided by teenagers with little experience or training in child care, older women balancing caring for your child with care of their own, and illegal immigrants whose off-the-books wages are often paid by women earning little more than the women they've hired.

Additionally, thousands of infants are cared for by relatives other than a parent. This is usually a convenient and loving arrangement, but research by the Families and Work Institute shows these children don't necessarily securely attach to a caregiver just because she's an aunt, grandmother, cousin, or other relative. This may be because caregivers who are relatives don't usually provide child care because they want to, or because they're trained for it, but because they need the money. As noted earlier, good child care outcomes are linked to caregivers who are both personally and professionally in-

Interview Questions: In-Home Child Care Provider

Be sure to ask the following questions of any candidates you're considering hiring to provide in-home caregiving to your child:

* How much education have you had? How many classes on child care or child development?

* How much hands-on experience have you had caring for young infants?

* How many jobs of this sort have you had, and how long did you typically remain in these positions?

* How old were the children in your care? How many were there?

* Why did you leave your last position?

* What do you like most about caring for infants? What do you like the least?

* Why are you interested in this job?

* Do you have any first aid training? Are you certified in infant CPR? (If not: Would you be willing to take such training at our expense if you are hired?)

* What would a typical day be like for my child in your care?

* Do you own a car and have a current driver's license?

* Have you ever been involved in a car accident or received a ticket for a moving violation? (Get details about these; also ask about car insurance and coverage)

* Do you smoke?

* Can you give me a list of people who will provide references for you, including your two most recent employers?

* What would you do if the baby cried for a long time without stopping? Ran a fever or broke out in a rash? Vomited? Fell?

vested in providing knowledgeable and developmentally appropriate care; this is rarely the case when extended family members assume child care responsibilities.

Nannies and private sitters might be well-trained in child development, or they might be high school dropouts with little background to prepare them for spending all day with a demanding infant. Even when an in-home caregiver is terrific—and many of them are—high turnover is a problem. No statistics exist to tell us just how big the problem is, however, since such arrangements tend to be unregulated.

Family child care. Family day care is used most frequently by parents of very young children. In fact, one-third of employed mothers with children under age 5 rely on care arrangements in which the caregiver takes care of several children in her own home. The actual definition of family day care varies, though it typically refers to a private home in which the resident provides care for four to six young children. Because many of these caregivers are drawn to child care so they can be at home with their own young children, some of the children they care for may be their own.

Regulations for family daycare homes vary widely from state to state. In some states, you can run a child care center from your home without a license as long as you keep the number of children you care for below a certain number. Often, though, the care provider's own children are not counted toward that maximum allowable number of children. So make sure *you're* doing the counting.

Family day care may or may not be licensed. In general, the quality of family day care tends to be merely adequate—neither hindering healthy child development nor providing the ideal environment for it, according to the National Child Care Staffing Study and many other research projects. There are, of course, exceptions at both extremes. Conditions in some family day care homes are nothing short

How to Conduct a Background Check

Before you hire someone to care for your child, you'll want to check his or her background carefully. Background checks may focus on one or more areas:

References provided by the candidate. If the woman you're considering hiring as your nanny worked for another family before coming to you, ask her former employer what her time with the family was like, what her strengths and weaknesses were, and why she left this job. Find out whether the caregiver was punctual, responsible, reliable, and creative, and whether the family had any concerns or desires for better performance in any area.

Criminal records. The law regarding the confidentiality and availability of criminal record checks varies from state to state. To be on the safe side, check with your attorney about whether you may obtain these in your state, and how.

Driving records. These are not considered to be confidential, and may be obtained from your state's Department of Motor Vehicles without the candidate's consent, typically for a fee.

Some general principles apply to conducting background checks:

✳ If you are checking out a child care center or hiring a nanny through a responsible agency, these checks will most likely have been conducted by them. Don't hesitate to ask, however, whether this has been done.

✳ Obtaining written consent from the candidate to conduct these checks (even those not demanding such consent) may protect you from later claims that her privacy was invaded. Should the candidate decline to give such consent, you may legally refuse to hire her for this reason.

✳ Don't assume her consent is a license to snoop through everything. Check only the things that are really pertinent to the hire. You don't really need to see her credit history, and previously filing for bankruptcy is not a legitimate reason to cross her off your list.

✳ You may hire a private investigator or an agency specializing in background checks to make these searches for you, but you'll probably save money by doing them yourself.

of appalling, while others are warm and appropriately stimulating, with responsive, loving, competent caregivers. The latter is more likely to be found in licensed homes, although there are no guarantees.

For instance, consider this story from Roberta, 27, a clinical psychologist. "I hurried back to my 4-month-old daughter as fast as the speed limit allowed after her first day in a licensed family day care home," she recalls. "I was envisioning this glorious re-

Interview Questions: Family Child Care Provider

Ask the candidate all of the relevant questions from the in-home caregiver list, plus the following:

* Why did you decide to become a day care provider?
* How many children will you be caring for at a time while my child is here? What are their ages?
* Will your own children be here when you're caring for my child? How old are they?
* Will they be handling any of my child's care?
* Are you licensed by the state?
* Have you applied for licensing? If you were turned down, why?
* What childproofing measures have you taken here?
* Are you familiar with storing, thawing, and using expressed breast milk?
* Do you have pets in the home, and if so, will my child have contact with them?
* Do you prefer to be paid by the day, week, or month?
* Do you charge additional fees for late pickup or early drop-off?
* Do you have a tax number or would you be willing to obtain one?
* Can you give me references—the names of people whose children you have cared for?

union with my happy baby, but instead I walked into the caregiver's house to find her watching television in the den and my Lucy wailing in a crib in another room. When I went to the kitchen to retrieve the bottles of breast milk I'd left for her, I found two of them untouched. The caregiver said she thought Lucy was too fat and didn't need so much milk. There was no question of ever going back again, and you can't even begin to imagine my guilt. But it was also a nightmare because we had to scramble for another caregiver."

Child care centers. About one-third of children in day care attend child care centers. Center care is the most popular form of care for children ages 3 to 5 years, but many centers also provide care for infants as young as 2 weeks. In most centers, infants are kept apart from the older children, spending most of their time with caregivers in a specially equipped "baby room."

Center care typically consists of group arrangements involving a dozen or more children. Settings vary, and include both for-profit arrangements (like national or regional chains such as KinderCare Learning Centers) and not-for-profit centers like those found in churches. Some employers provide on-site child care centers, while others subsidize their employee's child care expenses.

Some family day care homes that care for large numbers of children, called large or group family child care homes, may also be counted as child care centers and be required to meet state regulations pertaining to center care.

THE BUSINESS OF BABY CARE

Costs for day care vary widely across and even within geographic regions, depending on the type of care and the age of the child. But it's safe to say that quality child care is expensive. It has often been

Interview Questions: Center Care Provider

Ask the candidate all of the relevant questions from the previous two lists, plus the following:

* What kind of training do the staff members have in child development? Do they have infant CPR and first aid training?

* Are you licensed by the state?

* How many children attend the center at a given time, and what are their ages?

* How many caregivers work here?

* How many infants will be here, and how many caregivers work with them?

* Has the center ever been investigated for any problems?

* How long do staff members tend to stay here? What's the turnover rate?

* What fees do you charge for early drop-off or late pickup?

* Do you have an established procedure for regular parent/caregiver interaction?

* Do you bill by the day, the week, or the month? What is your tax number?

said that every 5 minutes your child spends being loved, watched over, protected, and cared for as a baby buys you an hour you don't have to worry when she's a teenager. So while quality care is expensive, there's no better investment you can make.

As a rule, the cost of child care drops as the child gets older, largely because the recommended staff to child ratios decline with the age of the child. In general, in-home, one-to-one care is more expensive than group care provided in either a center or family daycare setting. Also, infant care in cities typically costs more than in

Comparing Child Care Settings

Choosing the right care setting for you and your child means carefully evaluating the pros and cons of each option. Here are the main points to consider.

Child Care Setting	Advantages	Disadvantages
In-home Care	* Familiar setting * 1:1 caregiver/child ratio * Convenient for parents	* Most costly form of care * No backup if caregiver is ill or quits * Well-trained, experienced caregivers difficult to find * Employer must pay Social Security and other man-dated payments, including workman's compensation
Family Day Care	* Homelike setting, attractive for infants * Shared care keeps costs relatively low * Exposure to other children can provide social benefits	* No backup if caregiver is ill or quits * Least likely to be licensed * Exposure to other children can result in illnesses * Hours may not match parent's work hours
Center Care	* Shared care keeps costs relatively low * Backup staff for regular caregivers' illness or absence * Child-oriented environment * Provides social activities in group setting * Trained staff is likely * Costs related to taxes, insurance, etc., built into payments	* Least home-like setting * Highest staff turnover * Exposure to other children can result in illnesses * Rigid opening and closing times

small towns, suburbs, and rural areas, with infant care on the East and West Coasts typically costing more than care in the interior states.

THE UNDERGROUND ECONOMY

Hiring a child care provider for in-home or family day care adds another ball to your juggling act. Now you're not only a wife, mother, and employee, you're also an employer with responsibility for Social Security, Medicare, and unemployment insurance. Ignoring these responsibilities can be damaging. In 1993, attorney and mother of two, Zoey Baird, was nominated for the post of U.S. Attorney General. Her nomination was scuttled, however, when it was discovered that she had never paid Social Security taxes for the Peruvian couple who cared for her home and children.

Even if you're pretty sure you'll never be in line for the Attorney General's position, there are good reasons to play by the rules when it comes to your child care provider. If you pay her under the table, you face any or all of the following:

* Criminal penalties
* Inability to claim any child care-related expenses on your income taxes
* Having to pay back taxes and Social Security payments—with interest—if your caregiver files for them
* Inability to take advantage of any dependent care flexible spending accounts your employer offers

Your legal responsibilities include:

* Obtaining an employer ID number for federal and state tax payments. The federal number is obtained through the Internal Revenue Service, which you can reach at www.irs.gov or by phoning

(800) 829-3676. To obtain your state number, look under "Employment" in the government listings (usually the blue pages) in your telephone book.

* Setting up a payroll system for your caregiver. You need to keep track of income taxes, Social Security, and Medicare taxes if you pay your caregiver $1,300 or more per year (This is a 2003 figure.). To determine how much to pay, consult your accountant or use one of the online tax calculators at www.4homehelp.com/ChildFAQ.html or www.smartmoney.com.

* Verifying immigration status. If your caregiver is an immigrant, you are legally responsible for verifying her eligibility to work in the United States. Call the United States Bureau of Citizenship and Immigration Services at (800) 357-2099 and request an I-9 form, which will help to determine whether she can be hired legally. This form can also be downloaded for free from the Bureau's Web site. The easiest way to do this is to go to www.immigration.gov and use the site's A-Z index to look up "forms" for the download link, and "employment eligibility verification" to read the detailed instructions for the use of this form. You and your

What's a Dependent Care Account?

A dependent care account, or DCA, is an employer-offered benefit that enables you to pay your child care provider with pre-tax dollars. Such an account could save you 20 percent or more on your child care expenses by reducing your taxable income. Remember, though, if your employer offers this benefit, you can take advantage of it only if you are paying your child care provider legally and above board, and if both you and she complete the requisite paperwork accurately disclosing your child care expenses.

caregiver must each fill out the appropriate sections of the form, which you, as the employer, must then keep on file for 3 years after the date of hire, or 1 year after the caregiver leaves your employ, whichever is later.

Finally, keep thorough records. If you are uncertain of these procedures, consult an accountant or tax attorney.

FINDING CHILD CARE

There is plenty of child care available in the United States, but it's clear that only a relatively small portion of it is safe and appropriate for infants. Throw into the mix the need to find care that's affordable, that meets your schedule, and that's within reasonable proximity to your home and/or workplace, and it may begin to seem impossible to locate a care provider that's right for you and your family. Although about a third of parents find a caregiver within a week, the search can take months.

Yet the majority of women wait until they are in their third trimester of pregnancy before beginning to look for care; some wait until as late as the week before they return to work! Don't let this happen to you. There are numerous ways to gather information about available care, including:

Word of mouth. Parents are the ones with their fingers on the child care pulse in a community. Ask friends and acquaintances what you can expect to pay in your area, and what options are available. Parents also know the baby care scuttlebutt—who has a great caregiver, who had a bad experience.

The phone book. Look under both "child care" and "day care" in the yellow pages, and under the "information" section in the front pages of the book. Most states will have a listing for something like an "Infoline," which you can call to ask for a list of licensed caregivers in your area.

Work. Many employers maintain lists of licensed daycare centers and homes in your area, or provide access to child care resources that can help you find appropriate care.

Community. Churches and synagogues, senior centers, even the bulletin board in a baby clothes shop or a nursery school may put you on to a good caregiver.

Newspaper. Be careful here. Whether you're calling someone who has placed an ad offering child care services, or considering candidates who have answered *your* ad, you need to do some careful prescreening over the phone to weed out less stable or committed applicants. See Appendix C on page 239 for suggestions about what to ask before agreeing to interview a candidate obtained through a newspaper ad.

Resource and referral services. Organizations concerned with the licensing and improvement of child care choices often maintain links to local facilities that can assist you in your search. Again, Appendix C on page 239 has a list of some of these.

Universities and community colleges. If you're looking for flexible or part-time care, check with the psychology, child or early childhood development departments of local universities and community colleges. Ask department heads for recommendations and for lists of students who provide this type of service, or for a place where you can post your own ad.

INTERVIEWING AND SCREENING

When interviewing candidates or visiting potential child care centers, consider what kind of caregiver you want your baby to have, and what kind of experience you hope she'll have while you're at work.

Here are some of the bottom-line requirements to look for:

Caregiver's education. Caregivers should be well-educated, or at least trained in the basics of child development and how to optimize social, cognitive, and physical development.

Classroom size. If you are looking at family day care or center care, look for the appropriate caregiver/child ratios as described on page 174.

Environment. Babies should have an area of their own in which they can nap and play safely, away from older children. The environment should be clean and bright, with clear evidence that safety is a priority. Ask about and look for the following:

* Smoke alarms, fire extinguishers, and easily accessible emergency exits
* Securely blocked or plugged electrical outlets
* Age-appropriate toys (for instance, no tiny toys that can present choking hazards in the infant or toddler rooms)
* Stairways and open doorways blocked with baby gates
* Tables, bookcases, and lamps well secured so babies can't pull them over
* Drapery and blind cords well out of reach so children can't strangle themselves
* Sturdy cribs and playpens that meet current safety standards
* Emergency numbers (fire, police, poison control) posted by telephone
* Cupboard doors latched with safety locks
* No baby "walkers" (they present significant safety hazards)

Caregiver interaction. The most important element, of course, is the caregiver. She should be knowledgeable, warm, and responsive. Can she read your baby's verbal and non-verbal cues? Does

The Five Senses of a Child Care Setting

In your search for quality child care, make sure you spend some time in the caregiver's home or center before and after your child is enrolled. By using your five senses, you'll be able to discern quite a bit of information about the level of care your child will receive.

Look. Do caregivers and babies appear anxious, or happy, calm, and energetic? Are there opportunities for both quiet and stimulating activities? Are caregivers holding babies often and interacting with them appropriately? Do the caregivers wash their hands before and after diapering each child?

Listen. Are too many babies crying? Is the television blaring? Or is it *too* quiet, with infants bored and listless from having been left too long in a crib or infant seat?

Feel. Are edges of furniture and toys smooth and safe? Is the room too hot or too cold? Use your intuition: does the child care setting "feel right" to you, or does it make you uneasy?

Smell. Does the air smell of dirty diapers, sour milk or have other unpleasant odors? Or is it fresh and clean?

Taste. Take note of food-preparation areas and sanitary practices. Are formula and breast milk stored and heated safely? Is hand-washing before the preparation of food a routine practice?

---

she talk to him and hold him at appropriate times, yet give him space to explore when he needs to? Does she sit on the floor next to your baby on his blanket while you two talk, or does she sit stiffly in her chair opposite you without interacting with your child? Does she rush to embrace him, or does she patiently wait for the baby to approach her?

Caregiver continuity. Ask any potential caregiver how long she's been on the job and her plans for the future. In a center, ask about staff turnover—how long do most staff members stay at the center? Babies grieve over their losses just as older children and adults do.

Some departures are unavoidable, but a baby who loses three caregivers in 6 months may become wary, distrustful, and sad.

THE OTHER WOMAN

Almost every mother with a baby in child care worries about whether her child is eating right, being held and cuddled, being changed frequently, and being stimulated and talked to. She also worries about something else: "What if she gets mixed up about who her mother is? What if she loves the caregiver more than she loves me?"

"I worked so hard to find the best caregiver I could for my son Sam," says Caroline, 30, a bookstore manager. "And I was happy from the start with the family day care home he attends while I work at the store. He loves Mollie, the woman who cares for him and two other children in her home, and I feel safe and secure and trust her completely. So why do I feel this terrible little pang of jealousy every time I drop Sam off at her house and he squeals with glee as soon as he sees her?"

It's true that if a baby has too much variation in his care giving early in his life, he may not develop a strong sense of security, continuity, and predictability. Such an infant, when distressed, may seek out a parent or other caregiver but may not be able to derive as much comfort or emotional fuel as a more securely attached infant. Nor will this baby be able to separate as well or as comfortably as a more secure child, and will cling desperately to a parent without gaining much sense of security from the contact.

The good news, though, is that such confusion is the exception rather than the rule. Most children are adaptable enough to do two important things: become securely attached to not just two but to several important caregivers, and to do so without confusion over

Checking It Out: Before and After

It's almost a given that you will check out a day care center or family day care home before enrolling your baby, but not every parent knows what to look for. By consulting the resources listed in Appendix F on page 245, you'll find more information on what to include on your check-it-out list, but these are the basics:

* Are there the right number of caregivers for the number of babies in the setting? (According to experts, each caregiver should be responsible for no more than three infants, four toddlers, or five preschoolers at once.)

* Do you see evidence of appropriate childproofing?

* Is there a quiet area for sleeping and relaxing?

* Are babies being held for cuddling and feeding?

* Are children and caregivers happy and relaxed? Is there a reasonable level of calm, or does the atmosphere seem chaotic?

* Are caregivers washing their hands appropriately?

* Does the place please your five senses? Does it smell fresh, is there good air and lighting, are most babies cooing, babbling, or laughing instead of wailing or whining? Is the temperature right? If food or

who his parents are. Rest assured: By taking a well-planned family leave and spending time together as a family during your child's first few months of life, this secure sense of attachment among all three of you will grow and strengthen, and each of you will derive from it the resources you need to explore and take on the world.

KEEPING WHAT YOU HAVE

A BabyCenter.com poll conducted between 2001 and 2003 found that 74 percent of nearly 13,000 parents surveyed would use a video camera to film their child care worker, most without provocation or bottles are being prepared, do they appear to be fresh and appetizing, and stored safely?

* Do the caregivers seem happy to have you observing?

Similarly, once you've chosen a child care arrangement, continue to monitor it by asking all of the above questions and a few more:

* Does your baby seem happy to be with the caregiver?

* Does the caregiver welcome you if you pop in early or unexpectedly?

* Are children appropriately occupied with exploring toys or their surroundings, or engaged with the caregivers, or are they bored, crabby, or listless?

* Are there children in the setting whom you feel are too ill to be there? (Look for runny noses with green mucus; listen for bad coughs.)

* Does your caregiver want to know how the baby's night was when you arrive, and does she share information about his day when you come to pick him up?

* In general, do you feel comfortable with the way the arrangement is working out?

actual cause for suspicion. This raises the question: Why would you hire a child care worker you didn't feel you could trust? The reason, of course, is that high-quality child care is so hard to find; many parents are driven more by desperation than by choice. If you decide to use a camera, bear in mind that new technology means that any gifted hacker driving by your home with the right equipment can use it to spy on *you* (are you home? are your valuables?) if your surveillance equipment is of the more current wireless variety. Anecdotal reports also suggest that such a camera may pick up images from the surrounding area as well—you may end up with a charming video of your next-door-neighbor's baby.

Still, as this chapter notes, developing and trusting your own criteria, based not only on expert recommendations about ratios and training, but on your own instincts, can get you what you need. Keeping what you need, however, is just as important as finding quality day care in the first place. Making the child care relationship work takes three things: excellent communication; respect and professional treatment; and accommodations for the changes that will inevitably come as your baby grows older and has different developmental needs, or as your own work arrangements change.

Excellent communication. When you leave your baby with her caregiver before work, whether it's at your house, the caregiver's, or a child care center, take a few minutes to share with her anything that will make it easier for her to care for your child. Was the baby up all night teething? Did yesterday's strained spinach give her a rash? Is she *this* close to rolling over and needs to be watched with even greater care? The same is true of the end of the day. If your baby stays in a child care center in which eight parents are picking up babies and toddlers at the same time, don't make the caregiver's life crazier by trying to have a conference every afternoon. But do talk briefly with her about your child's day, and whether there's anything you need to know.

Respect and professional treatment. This means showing up on time at the end of the day, paying your child care provider on time, and staying up to date on any paperwork related to her employment. If you have a home day care provider or an in-home caregiver, provide occasional gifts that benefit both of you: a class in infant first aid/CPR, a subscription to a child care magazine or journal. Remember, too, that you aren't just paying her to provide a service—she's an important person in your life and the life of your child. Get to know her. What does she like to do in her time off? A more personal gift on her birthday and at the holidays, or sometimes, just because, shows that you recognize her as a person, not just a service provider.

Ch-ch-ch-changes. Change is a normal—if often disruptive—reality in any family's life. The nanny who was ideal for your babe-in-arms may not be as comfortable with a growing (scrambling, climbing) toddler. Carolyn, 32, was thrilled with how her family day care provider met every need of her infant daughter Abby, but as Abby grew, Carolyn began to feel that the program was no longer right for her. "When Abby was just on breast milk that I supplied every day, her diet was fine, but once she switched to solid food, I realized the caregiver was letting her snack on a lot of junk food. I was also coming in after work and finding Abby watching television, way too often. I think that as she grew more mobile, the caregiver—an older woman who really did love her—was just too tired to keep up with her activity, and used the television as a means of curbing her exploration." In the end, Carolyn decided to put Abby in a toddler program run by their town, where the food was more nutritious and the caregivers were more likely to encourage active play and exploration.

SOOTHING SEPARATION ANXIETY

Physical growth isn't the only thing that changes so rapidly in the early years. Your child's awareness of your absence—and her response to it—changes, too. The newborn who was asleep most mornings when you dropped her off becomes an 8-month-old who can't bear to say goodbye. Suddenly, what was a pretty low-key part of your day becomes stressful with a capital S.

That's what Karen, a 45-year-old data systems administrator, found when her daughter, Jannie, turned 9 months. "I had her in my arms as I was chatting with Suzie, our nanny, before work," she recalls. "Then, like always, I gave Jannie a kiss and a little squeeze, and handed her to Suzie." But this time something was different. "She was like the incredible stretching baby—the nanny was holding her in her arms, and I was moving away, but Jannie managed to still hold onto me. Holding on with an iron grip, and *wailing*. Not one tear had this little girl ever shed in the mornings, and suddenly she was crying as if her heart would break. Well, naturally, I started to cry, too—even Suzie was tearing up." Yet when Karen phoned from her car 10 minutes after the devastating goodbye scene, Suzie laughed and reported that Jannie was happily sitting up in a bird's nest of pillows, playing with a pile of pop-beads, quite tear-free.

Episodes of separation anxiety, which typically raises its head for the first time around 8 or 9 months, are perfectly normal—but they can be tough on all three of you: parent, child, and child care provider. They occur as your child becomes aware of you as a separate person, and so is more aware of your departure. She'll settle down again after a few such episodes, although you may get a repeat when she turns 18 months and then again at 3 years—or if she experiences any stressful life events, such as an illness or a move. To get through these heart-wrenching moments:

Remember she's okay. You have a child care provider you trust, one with whom your child is safe and happy. Call later, if you want to, to make sure she is happy again. Most of the time the answer will be "She quit crying as soon as you were out of sight."

Go for quick goodbyes. Don't linger. If your child senses any ambivalence on your part, it will only make the separation worse. Kiss her, hug her and hand her to your caregiver. Then go, cheerfully waving as you do.

Give her something special. A photo of you, a special teddy bear, a scarf with a lingering smell of your cologne, or a blanket will do. Within the next few months, she'll probably settle on a special toy or two that will be her "lovey," her security object. Encourage the use of these, as they will help her bridge the hours apart from you.

Don't ask permission. Don't say, "I'm going to go now, OK?" What if she says no?

Don't apologize. Telling her how sorry you are that you have to leave her in day care will backfire some day. Cheerfully tell her that you are going to your work, and that day care is her work.

BUYING AN EXPERIENCE

Experts emphasize that when you make a choice about child care, you aren't just purchasing a service like hiring someone to deliver your diapers or dry clean your clothes. In choosing a child care setting, you're choosing an environment in which your child will likely spend a significant portion of his or her time over the next several years.

There's no question that the nature and quality of this environment can have a profound and persistent impact on your child's development and health, as well as your level of stress and work performance.

The head start you gave your baby during your maternity leave, even though it may not have been as long as you would have liked, should be followed up by a day care experience that continues to build on the loving-kindness, warmth, and consistency of care you provided during those first weeks of life.

KEYS TO KEEPING THE BALANCE

Because there are no federal child care standards in the United States, and state standards range from appropriate to woefully inadequate, it is up to parents to set their own standards and to research and monitor their child care choices to ensure they're upheld.

Most child care falls into three categories: in-home care, family child care, and center care. Licensing is no guarantee of quality, but is more likely to be associated with good care.

Higher-quality day care leads to better outcomes in terms of health and safety, behavior, school readiness, and cognitive and social development.

Much of the American day care economy exists underground, but there are significant benefits to handling all child care transactions within the framework of tax, business, and immigration laws.

In spite of all the bad news about child care in America, parents with high standards who are diligent about searching for quality care—and who can afford to pay for it—can find what they're looking for.

10

THE COMEBACK KID

When the Web site Babycenter.com asked new mothers about their post-baby lives, 62 percent of the 10,539 respondents said they had returned to work following family leave, or, if still on leave, had definite plans to do so. Yet nearly 40 percent of these women called the return "wrenching." Just 15 percent said it was "satisfying."

How well your return goes depends in large part on how well you planned your leave and to what extent the leave itself met your expectations and needs. For instance, maybe despite your deep-rooted love for your baby, you're bored out of your gourd and feeling isolated at home. You may love your job and miss the excitement and sense of purpose you get from your work there and can't wait to get back.

Or maybe all thoughts of returning to work flew out of your head with that first toothless grin. But no matter how much you've reworked the budget, it's just not financially feasible for you to stay home. So you're depressed and resentful about your return.

Regardless of how you feel now, the most important thing to remember is that the transition back to work is an ongoing process, not a now-I'm-on-leave/now-I'm-back event. Returning to work, getting up to speed on new projects, and catching up on the latest gossip and the neglected e-mail will take a while. This is particularly true if you, like many new moms, ease slowly back into work with a part-time schedule instead of leaping in with a splash.

There's another important aspect of this transition to consider here: you. You are not the same person now that you were when you last sat at your desk or stood at your cash register or puzzled over your microscope. Now you're a mother. This will affect everything you do. Your priorities have been shaken and stirred, and, in the process, thoroughly rearranged. Wherever your job stood on your personal commitment scale pre-baby, you can bet it will be at least a rung lower than it was a few short weeks ago.

You may even be toying with the idea of quitting, a fantasy of nearly every new mother at some time during her maternity leave. It may be only a passing consideration, or one you spend much of your leave obsessing over. That's what Darla, a 31-year-old chef, discovered.

Two weeks after her son was born, she was hit with the bolt of mother love she'd only read about. "I was wide awake in the middle of the night and tiptoed into his room in the dark. I started shaking from head to toe, and scooped him up out of his crib and held him. I knew at that minute that I would die for this child, that the center of the universe had suddenly shifted, and that I loved him with every fiber of my being. It was an incredible moment, one that changed everything for me. I also knew that I still loved my job and would go back to it within a few months, but now I knew I would always be at the center of a tug-of-war between work and motherhood."

Making either decision—to quit or stay—isn't easy, but the information in this chapter will help.

DECIDING WHEN TO RETURN

When *can* you go back to work? The longer you can stay with your baby during these first months, the better off she or he will be, and most women find that they would like to take as much time off as they can. Parents are the center of an infant's universe, and the more time they can spend together, the stronger the baby's sense of stability and safety will be. This, in turn, forms the foundation on which all human development is based. The longer you can spend together, interacting, learning to read each others' signals, finding your place as partners in this dance of mutual and growing understanding, the more secure your baby will be.

There are women who return to work within 2 weeks of giving birth. This is not advisable from either the mother's or the baby's standpoint. But again, making sure you can provide materially for your baby is also an important consideration. At the very minimum, a 6-week leave (the length typically defined as an appropriate disability leave following an uncomplicated vaginal delivery) would allow most women a chance to heal physically—though most at this stage are still somewhat fatigued; some may still be bleeding.

If you *must* return to work at this stage, speak with your health care provider about whether this is medically advisable. In some cases you may be able to get a few more weeks of leave for medical reasons. Few, if any moms have ever said, "Gosh, if only I'd taken less time off after my baby was born!" A 2002 *Parenting* magazine poll notes that the average leave taken among respondents lasted $10^1/_2$ weeks. Roughly 26 percent of the 3,120 moms taking part in the poll expressed regret that they hadn't taken more time off.

INTRODUCING YOUR BABY
TO CHILD CARE

I'll be back. At least, that's what you told them. Now, like General MacArthur or the Terminator, it's time to prepare for your return. Ideally, by the time you're ready to return to work you've already arranged for quality childcare you feel comfortable with, following all the recommendations in chapter 9. This is a major step you must take to smooth your transition from mom to working mom.

But don't wait until your first day back at work for your child's first day at daycare. Start with a few trial runs. A couple of weeks before you plan to return to work, ask your caregiver to come in for a day, or take your child to the new daycare center or family home.

It will be difficult leaving him that first time, but at least you can go home and cry instead of having to head right for work. Take advantage of the break to do something for you. Get a great new back-to-work haircut and color. Read something more thought provoking than the brochure that came with your new crib. Restore your sleep-deprived brain cells with a nap.

If the first outing goes well, try leaving your baby a few more times before your official return-to-work. It doesn't have to be all

Beyond the Baby Blues: Postpartum Depression

Most women experience the baby blues, short periods of weepiness and strong emotions that last for a few days after giving birth. But one in 1,000 experiences a more serious form of the blues called postpartum depression, or PPD. Symptoms include anxiety, insomnia, unexplained crying, loss of appetite, difficulty concentrating, lack of self-esteem or self-worth, feelings of guilt, and lack of initiative.

Physical exhaustion, discomfort, and inadequate support all play a role in bringing on PPD; so can genetic factors. If you've had PPD after a previous pregnancy, it can recur with greater intensity, and if you were diagnosed with depression prior to becoming pregnant, your risk for developing PPD may be increased. (Make sure your health care provider is aware of this history.)

If you think you're having a problem with PPD, call your doctor immediately. Left untreated, PPD can lead to postpartum psychosis, a condition in which you might endanger your baby and/or yourself.

day; in fact, if you're nursing, you may want only a 3-hour break. But the experience will be good practice for getting you and your baby ready in the morning, help your breastfed child get used to a bottle of expressed milk (or formula if you aren't able to breastfeed during the day at work), and provide valuable peace of mind on your first day back at work.

BREASTFEEDING BASICS

With the introduction to childcare out of the way, you can turn your attention to breastfeeding. Whether you nurse your baby or feed him formula—and, if you decide to nurse, how long you do—are personal decisions. As a country, we fall far behind in numbers of women who choose to breastfeed; in 1997, for instance, the United States had one of the lowest rates of breastfeeding in the entire world. Yet the American Academy of Pediatrics recommends all infants be breastfed "well into the second year."

The Academy's recommendation is based on the numerous health benefits of prolonged nursing. Studies find that breastfed babies have fewer ear infections, respiratory illnesses, and episodes of diarrhea or constipation. Breastfeeding also reduces a child's risk of asthma, allergies, diabetes, and obesity. For you, long-term breastfeeding lowers your risk of premenopausal breast cancer. The American Academy of Pediatrics recommends that infants should be nursed for at least 12 months. A Yale University study released in 2002 says that for every year a woman breastfeeds over a lifetime, her risk of breast cancer is lowered by 4 percent.

Plus, breast milk is best for your baby. No formula company has yet devised a fluid as perfectly suited for a human infant's nutritional and developmental needs. Breast milk is more easily digested than cow's milk or formula, containing more than 50 known immunological factors that protect infants against illness and disease (and many more that haven't been discovered yet). If your baby is healthier, your health care costs will be lower, and you'll miss less work—a definite plus where your boss and coworkers are concerned.

Breastfeeding (once you've got the hang of it) is also easier and less expensive than bottle feeding. There's no formula to purchase (saving an estimated $900 a year), mix, store, and heat, and no bottles or other equipment to wash. And, once you and your baby are firmly established in your nursing routine, there's nothing wrong with expressing a bottle of milk for your partner, mother, or other caregiver to give the baby.

Having said all that, if you try breastfeeding and feel it's just not for you, or you have problems nursing that make every feeding a frustrating, tearful time, that's okay, too. You are *not* a bad mother!

For instance, consider what happened to Jennifer. Her daughter, Alice, was born 4 weeks prematurely. Jennifer tried to nurse her, but from the beginning, Alice had a weak and inefficient sucking response and had trouble latching onto Jennifer's nipple. Even a lactation consultant couldn't help. When a checkup revealed Alice had *lost* weight since her previous exam, the pediatrician gently but firmly advised Jennifer to try formula. "You gave it a great try, Jennifer," she said. "And we want moms to nurse. But we also want moms and babies to be happy and healthy and comfortable together, and you guys are miserable over this. Give this baby a bottle and relax." By the next visit, Alice's weight was just right for her length, and she and Jennifer—who felt both happier and more secure—were enjoying the cozy, warm interactions they had at feeding time.

BREASTFEEDING PREPARATIONS BEFORE YOU RETURN TO WORK

Some women give up breastfeeding—or never start—because they think they can't combine nursing with working outside the home. What they don't know is that with just a little effort, you won't have to start your baby on formula. You can continue to nurse when the two of you are together, and to provide your child with enough stored breast milk for use at day care. The key is building up a good supply of expressed milk *before* your leave ends, so you've always got some in the bank.

The first step is buying or borrowing a good-quality breast pump. Don't mess with those small manual hand pumps—they are uncomfortable, inefficient, mean little devices. You want a mechanized pump that's small enough to carry back and forth to work. You might be able to rent one from your health care provider, hospital, Visiting Nurse Association office, or the nearest chapter of La Leche League. If you plan to nurse for a year or more, it may be less expensive in the long run to purchase your own pump. See Appendix G on page 246 for breastfeeding resources.

Now you want to build up your backup milk supply. That means building up your internal milk supply, and the only way to do that is with a classic supply-and-demand approach. Continue to nurse frequently while you're home, but about a month before you return to work, begin pumping some extra milk. Good times to do this are first thing in the morning before your baby wakes up, or after she nurses. Don't worry if you feel like you're not getting much; the more you pump, the more your body will make. And don't worry about shortchanging your baby; she'll keep sucking until she gets what she needs.

At first, hooking up your breasts to an automatic breast pump can feel awkward and embarrassing (as if you should be saying "moo"). But soon you'll be a pro, able to read while the machine quietly and efficiently pumps out the best food for your baby in about 15 minutes.

Store this milk in freezer-quality bags in quantities of no more than 2 or 3 ounces; you don't want it to go to waste by thawing more than you can use within 24 hours. Leave a little space for the frozen milk to expand, and write the date on each bag with a laundry marker. By the time you return to work, you should have a good supply built up. Be sure you use the oldest bags first. They should be defrosted under warm running water or in a bowl of warm water, never in the microwave. Breast milk can be safely stored in the refrigerator for up to a week; frozen milk, stored in the back (the coolest part) of your freezer, will keep for up to 6 months.

Start introducing bottles of expressed milk a couple of weeks before you return to work. Because many breastfed babies refuse to take a bottle from their mother, enlist the support of your partner, mother, or the babysitter if she has already started working for you. Don't be in the room the first few times they offer your baby breast milk in a bottle—babies seem to find this confusing.

BREASTFEEDING ON THE JOB

So your freezer is filled with little bags of breast milk and it's time to return to work. You have several options. You can decide to continue breastfeeding just in the morning, at night, and on weekends, and let your childcare provider give your baby formula once your expressed milk runs out. Or you can try to keep your baby on breast milk only, maintaining your supply during the day, and, of course, pumping at work. Here's how.

Find a place to pump. If your boss suggests you pump in the bathroom, firmly refuse the offer. Bathrooms are uncomfortable and

The Breastfeeding-on-the-Job Survival Kit

Here's what you'll need to combine work and breastfeeding:

* Electric breast pump. Make sure it's small, portable, includes a carrying case, and has an efficient but quiet motor. Prices range from just under $100 to upwards of $300; models are often available for rent from your local Visiting Nurse Association or La Leche League chapter.

* Small, clean hand towel; washcloth or gentle wipes

* Small cooler with nonspill freezer packs for transporting milk

* Plastic nursing bottles or sturdy ziplock bags labeled with your name and date

* A bag with a carrying strap for storing and transporting the following:

   A photo of your baby (looking at it can stimulate letdown)

   Something to do while you're nursing, such as a book or portable music player; books on tape or CD are great for this and can often be checked out at the library

   A supply of washable or disposable breast pads

   A clean shirt (just in case) or a sweater you can put on to hide leakage

* If you plan to store expressed breast milk in the office refrigerator during the day, it's a good idea to keep the bottles or bags in a lunch box, brown bag, or other container with your name on it. It's disconcerting (for both you and your coworker) to find your milk has been mistaken for coffee creamer.

unsanitary (would you want to eat food prepared in the bathroom?), not to mention there's no privacy and it's demeaning. If you have your own office with a door you can close, you've got it knocked. Otherwise seek out the employee lounge, an empty office, or an unused conference room. Some highly enlightened firms such as

Daimler-Chrysler, Dupont and Rodale provide lactation rooms in which a woman can pump her milk in comfort. Six states—California, Connecticut, Hawaii, Illinois, Minnesota, and Tennessee—have laws guaranteeing a woman time to pump at work. Georgia law specifically allows, but does not require, employers to make provisions for women to pump at work. The state of Washington not only allows (but does not require) employers to accommodate nursing mothers when they return to work, it also provides an incentive by allowing them to advertise themselves as "infant friendly" companies. And it is not illegal in any state to breastfeed in public.

Keep a regular schedule. In addition to pumping in the morning after your baby's feeding, you'll want to pump once or twice a day at work. If possible, pump at times when your baby would normally nurse. If you're fortunate to live in one of the enlightened states mentioned above, or have a compassionate and flexible employer, you can most likely adhere to such times. If things are a little more structured or rigid in your office, you may have to use your coffee break and/or lunch times to pump. If your job requires a lot of travel, you will have to get creative—pump in a lounge or empty office when you visit sympathetic clients, or, as a last resort, park discreetly and pump in your car.

Dress for easier access. Wear tops you can pull up, or tops or dresses with hidden front openings. Button-front blouses are not as optimal, as they tend to expose more skin than just a breast; if you find that you need access in a button-front blouse, unbuttoning from the bottom up may be more discreet than unbuttoning from the collar down. Breast leakage is inevitable—stock up on breast pads. If you leak through, turn your blouse or tee-shirt around or slip on a jacket or cardigan. Better yet, keep a couple of extra go-with-anything tops at your office to change into in case of leaks, or keep a sweater on hand to pull on over a wet blouse.

REJOINING THE WORK FORCE AS A NEW MOM

So you've got daycare and breastfeeding under control. Now it's time to turn your attention to the professional side—your actual return to the workplace. If you've been keeping up with the folks at work, either formally or informally, you're one step ahead. You're aware of any big events or serious issues affecting your company. You've stayed in the loop and know the important professional gossip. You've kept up with the industry news.

Check in a week or two before your official return date. Use your judgment to decide whether it's best to do this on the phone or in person, but at least make personal voice contact—don't try to do this by e-mail or fax. Fill your boss in on how you've kept in touch with the office, and get brought up to date on what's been happening during your absence. Learn what she thinks are the most important changes that have occurred and any crises you should be aware of.

Find out if anyone at work is harboring anger or resentment towards you because you've been away. Research shows that this is a typical reaction among coworkers who feel they've been inconvenienced or had to work harder because of your absence. Do what you can to defuse these feelings ahead of time. For instance, send the people who have been covering for you a written note (copied to their supervisor) thanking them for their help. Here's an example.

Beth—I wanted to take a moment to thank you for your sensitive handling of the Allied account while I've been away. I recently had an e-mail from Jocelyn, Allied's human resources director, letting me know how smoothly you guided their incentive plan development. I hope you don't mind that I've sent a copy of that message to be put in your employee file. Thanks again, Georgia

211

Food can go a long way toward soothing ruffled feathers. Bring in a dozen doughnuts on your first day back, or treat your coworkers to pizza for lunch as another sign of your gratitude.

Here are some other tips to make your return more pleasurable than stressful.

＊ Tell supervisors and a few coworkers your return date. Give clients a date that's one week later than your actual return date; this will give you time to get fully back in the swing of things before you make contact with them.

＊ Don't make your first day back at work a Monday. If you do, it will be the longest work week of your life. Try starting back on a Wednesday or Thursday—2 or 3 days is a good length of time to get your work legs back.

＊ Try arranging your partner's or spouse's leave time so just as you're returning to work, he's starting his leave. Your first day of separation from your child will be easier if you know she's staying with her other parent instead of a child care provider you may not completely trust yet.

Yessir, That's My Baby

In all but a few work environments, coming in a week or so before your return to show off the fruits of your labors (literally) is a rite of passage. Don't just drop in with the new baby, though, unless your workplace is run quite informally. Instead, call ahead and make plans to bring the baby by to visit your colleagues during lunch, or at the end of the day when work is winding down. Or make arrangements to have lunch outside the office with several office friends at a baby-friendly restaurant, meeting them at the office 20 or 30 minutes before you go out.

REDEFINING THE STANDARD

The *Parenting* magazine survey cited earlier in this chapter notes that 84 percent of working mothers who return to work after family leave say they didn't lose any ground professionally during their leave. So don't panic if at first it feels like you've been gone for years, or if there's a new face or two in the crowd. You'll have everything back under control quickly.

"I took some ribbing when I came back after a 3-month leave," says Sally, 35, an actuary for an insurance company. "But I also heard several complaints from people who felt they'd been victimized because I'd been away. I should have just blown them off, but I ended up feeling so guilty that they had to work hard that I really knocked myself out trying to be the perfect, overachieving, super-employee. I wore myself out!"

Don't be like Sally. While it's tempting to think you have to prove something to your employer and yourself, the sooner you get over this superwoman syndrome, the better. You can be Employee of the Month *next* month, okay?

The best way to reconnect in the workplace is to simply deliver the goods. Do your work, meet your goals, but don't make yourself insane trying to catch up on the 3 months of work you missed. Here's a trick: Most offices measure success in terms of how hard it *appears* someone is working. Start redefining this standard by substituting success and productivity for hours logged at the desk. If your worth at the office was judged before your pregnancy, implicitly or explicitly, by the number of hours you worked, if your office's credo is "she who dies with the most overtime wins," you will have your work cut out for you.

You may find, however, that you aren't quite the same *kind* of employee you were before, particularly if you have opted for a less traditional work arrangement. You are likely to be more productive in less time, but this isn't always as visible to your employer as when you're physically present in the office. If you're telecommuting, working part time, or job sharing, you may feel that you suffer for the lack of face time. Here are some ways around this.

Produce like crazy. Just get the job done, well and quickly.

Get some face time defined in your schedule. Even if you do 90 percent of your work from home, make sure you get into the office on a regular basis for face-to-face meetings with your manager. How often depends on your boss's schedule and your own. Ask how often she'd like to meet with you.

Focus on the bottom line. Avoid giving the impression you've changed your work schedule for your baby. Although this may be the main reason for switching to a more flexible work arrangement, don't keep reminding your supervisor of this. Frame it as an efficient, cost-effective way for you to get your work done faster and more productively, thus benefiting the company.

Provide tangible reminders of your value. On a regular basis, provide written documentation on what you're working on, focusing on what you've accomplished since the last report.

Invite regular reviews. Every quarter, ask your supervisor for feedback. Is she satisfied with your arrangement? Are there any lingering concerns? What can you do to address them? Then act on her suggestions.

You'll also find that parenting teaches you to be incredibly efficient. Most working mothers quickly develop a whole new tool kit of survival techniques and learn to compress large tasks or groups of tasks into a manageable amount of time. You can follow their lead with these tips:

Multitask. To the extent possible, divide tasks into those that require you to be at your desk, and those that you can take with you to work on during quiet times outside of the office. For example, page through industry publications while you're stuck in traffic. Sort mail while you're on the phone. Have meetings over lunch or breakfast.

Screen out distractions. Close your door when you're working hard, and avoid areas where you tend to get bogged down in long conversations, such as the water cooler. You don't have to be rude or anti-social, but restricting your socializing to a few minutes at the coffee machine in the morning will enable you to get out—and back to your baby—earlier in the evening.

Avoid time-wasting activity. If people drift into your office to chat, stand up while you talk with them—they'll leave sooner. If there's a social event at the office that you don't really have to attend, put in an appearance, convey your greetings to the birthday boy, then slip out and get back to work.

Work through minor infirmities. A headache that might have sent you packing in the old PB (pre-baby) days may be a triviality now.

Fight fatigue. Many of the self-care tips—eating right, exercising, drinking plenty of water, using stress busters like yoga or meditation—you learned during your pregnancy will continue to see you through the sleepless nights of motherhood.

Remember your motivation. As a new parent, who has more to work for now?

Know that documentation is your friend. If it's appropriate to your job and your corporate culture, provide your supervisor with a concise report within a week of your return to the job. Thank her for her support in helping you to make a smooth transition to and from the workplace, and add some specific notes to help bring her up to date on each of the projects you're working on.

THE WORKING MOTHER'S WORKING HOURS

Driven largely by parents interested in better balancing work and family life, businesses in the United States are increasingly likely to offer alternatives to traditional work arrangements, including part-time, flextime, and telecommuting options. This is especially true of companies employing a large proportion of women and part-time workers, but firms of all sizes and configurations are beginning to be more sensitive to the family needs of their workers. As a new parent, make it your job to find out about any such arrangements your company offers, and consider if any of the following might be right for you.

PART-TIME OR FLEXTIME SCHEDULES

When the *Parenting* magazine poll cited earlier asked women about the type of work arrangement they returned to after having a baby, 8 percent said they returned to the same job they'd held before, but shifted from a full-time to a part-time arrangement. Another 8 percent returned to their old job on a flextime basis.

Flextime is one of the fastest growing job options in the country today. Put simply, flextime is a benefit that allows you some flexibility in the hours you work. Instead of coming in from 9 to 5 every day, you might start work at 7:30 A.M., eat lunch at your desk, and make it home by 3. Or you may work 3 long and 2 short days. The Department of Labor reported in 2003 that roughly 29 million full-time workers, nearly 29 percent of the work force, take advantage of flextime's scheduling advantages. Compare that to 1991, when just 15 percent of American workers had a flextime option.

Willene, 34, loves the flexibility this option provides. Her boss at the garden center requires only that she inform him at the beginning of each month what hours she plans to work. Because she has an infant daughter and a son in first grade, she starts her day at 10 A.M. (her workplace opens at 8:30) after putting her son on the school bus, dropping her daughter off at the day care center, and swinging by the gym for a quick morning workout. Willene's husband, Bart, works for a package delivery service from 6 A.M. until 2 P.M., so he picks up the baby, meets their son's bus after school, spends the afternoon with the children, and starts dinner.

Other flex arrangements permit employees to work fewer, yet longer days a week, like four 10-hour days.

Job-sharing arrangements provide a different type of flexibility. Carol, 26, and Jenna, 30, paired up for a job share at the convalescent hospital where they work as nutritionists. Carol works full days

Who Offers What?

The Families and Work Institute's Business Work-Life Study surveyed 1,057 for- and not-for profit companies with 100 or more employees about their family-friendly benefits. Here's what they found.

Benefit Offered	Percentage of Companies Offering It
Time off for school/child care functions	88
Gradual return to work after family leave for childbirth or adoption	81
Periodic changes in starting and quitting times	68
Occasional work from home	55
Transition from full-time to part-time at same pay rate	57
Job sharing	37.5
Regular work from home or other off-site work	33
Changes in starting and quitting times on a daily basis	24

on Mondays and Tuesdays and until 1:00 P.M. on Wednesdays. At noon on Wednesdays, Jenna comes in, confers with Carol about the patients she's working with, and finishes out the week. On Monday mornings, Carol speaks by phone with the dietician who fills in on the weekends.

Carol used to work full-time at the hospital, but midway through her family leave realized that she wasn't comfortable putting her baby in full-time day care. Jenna was hired specifically to complete the job share partnership. Other job share arrangements may involve alternate days or weeks, and it is not unheard of for job share partners to share child care, as well.

TELECOMMUTING

Advances in technology that allow easy communication between a traditional workplace and employees performing most or all of their duties off-site make telecommuting, (sometimes called teleworking) possible. Those who telecommute successfully stress that this kind of work is not necessarily easier than working at the office. In fact, if you're someone who thrives on human contact, works better with supervision, and has a tendency to get distracted when the boss is away, telecommuting probably isn't for you.

Be aware, also, that you will still require child care support if you work from home. But telecommuting may enable you to spend more time with your baby by cutting out commuting time and improving your efficiency. Telecommuters report that, on average, it takes them an hour less each day to complete their daily tasks than it takes their counterparts in traditional work arrangements—a time savings of close to 6 weeks a year. Additionally, companies save money though reduced absenteeism, improved job retention, and fewer facility-related costs, such as heating and cooling, parking, and rent. Overall, 83 percent of workers who responded to an International Teleworker Association and Council 2001 poll reported that they are more satisfied with both their jobs and their personal lives since they began telecommuting.

Before proposing a telecommuting arrangement for some or all of your job duties, make sure it's right for you by answering the following questions:

* Can your duties be fulfilled away from the office?
* Would working from home negatively affect your interactions with clients and vendors?
* Do you work well independently and have good time management skills?
* Do you have the self-discipline required to stay on task, keep work and home commitments separate, stay away from the refrigerator, the television, and your personal e-mail until your jobs for the day are completed?
* Do you have excellent communication skills? These are essential for efficiently maintaining contact with your supervisor and coworkers.
* Are you technologically literate? There's no help desk in your house.

If you're convinced that telecommuting is a good option for you, check out the resources listed in Appendix H on page 247.

WORKING FROM HOME

If you work from home, you are still working, so unless your job is something like running your own family day care home, you will need at least part-time child care for your own baby. This doesn't entirely defeat the purpose, though, since you'll most likely have in-

Is Working at Home Right for You?

While some women crave unlimited time at home with their infants, other women feel they are more fulfilled—and, ultimately, better mothers—when they have a satisfying work life outside of the home. To determine if your personality is suited to staying at home full-time, take the following quiz.

1. I'm the kind of worker who . . .
   a. likes to be guided in what tasks I do and the pace at which I complete them.
   b. is self-motivated with respect to setting an agenda and meeting deadlines.

2. I thrive on . . .
   a. a busy, humming work atmosphere and the company of my co-workers.
   b. a quiet, solitary place to work.

3. My attitude toward taking a risk at work is . . .
   a. I don't think my boss would like it, and that's just fine with me.
   b. bring it on!

4. When I get stuck for ideas or find myself in a crisis, I . . .
   a. immediately turn to a co-worker or a supervisor for help.
   b. like to figure out for myself what to do next or how to find the answer I need.

5. I need to know that a paycheck is . . .
   a. absolutely positively going to be in my hand by Friday.
   b. out there somewhere, if I work hard enough and use good business sense.

finitely more flexibility than you had when you were in someone else's employ.

STAYING AT HOME FULL TIME

Thinking of staying home for a while? You're not alone. Roughly 4 out of 10 women who take family leave after birth or adoption

6. The idea of self-promotion makes me . . .
   a. cringe.
   b. start taking notes about business cards and advertising, and making lists of people with whom I can network.

7. I have enough financial resources to let me try an at-home career for . . .
   a. 45 minutes.
   b. 6 months, if I live carefully.

8. The product or service I'd offer in my work-from-home is . . .
   a. hmm . . . I'm sure I'll think of something.
   b. one I can easily offer from here, and for which there is an established demand or a demonstrable need.

9. If I never have to wear pantyhose again . . .
   a. I'll feel naked!
   b. it will be too soon.

10. I have an important skill worth money to others, and . . .
   a. I'm sure I'll figure out the business end eventually.
   b. good management, accounting, and contract negotiation skills.

If you chose mostly the "a" responses, it's a good idea to start researching the mechanics of working from home before you write out your resignation. Appendix H on page 247 offers a number of resources to help you get started, even if you're starting from scratch.

If you answered mostly with the "b" response, you'll be on your way much sooner, but the same resources will be helpful. Look first (and look well)—leap later.

choose not to return to the workplace right away. "Why did I have my baby girl if I'm just going to turn her over to someone else to raise?" laments 38-year-old Ellen, who left her 9 to 5 secretarial position to work at home as a medical transcriptionist.

While being a stay-at-home parent is hands-down the most difficult job you'll ever do, it's also the most important. And although it's exhausting, much of the stress that comes with balancing employment *and* mothering will be absent.

Of course, that's just replaced with other stresses, such as financial. Before you quit your job, ask yourself if you can really afford to stay home.

Remember the budget worksheets you completed in the first chapter of this book, when you were trying to find extra income to pay for an unpaid family leave? A similar exercise will help you decide whether you can afford to leave your job and become a stay-at-home mom. Add up child care costs; commuting costs such as gas and other car expenses, train fare, tolls, and parking; and other work-related costs, such as professional clothing or uniforms, eating lunch out, and buying more convenience foods for dinner (or eating out more) because you're too tired to cook. Now consider the tax implications of your working; does your salary put you and your husband in a higher tax bracket? Subtract these work-related costs from your take-home salary to see how much you're *really* earning. Then, see if there are other areas in your life where you can economize to make up for any remaining salary.

You also need to consider your benefits. If your job is the one that comes with the best health insurance, find out if your husband can provide the necessary coverage through his job. (Alternatively, of course, you may both discover that the best option is for your husband to stay home with the baby.)

In the end, you want to figure out how much it will cost you *not* to work. The final figure may surprise you. And keep in mind that the real reason many parents decide to stay home has more to do with those benefits you can't put a price on. Just imagine, never having to wear pantyhose again! And, oh, yeah, being with that beautiful baby.

CHOOSING A NEW JOB

Maybe the time you had away from your job made you realize that you don't want to return to it, but you still want to work. You need a new job! The difficulty lies in interviewing while you're home with a new baby. You also need to be aware of any liability you may incur by changing employers instead of returning directly to the employer from which you took your family leave. Most leaves, of course, are unpaid, but if your employer paid for all or part of your leave (other than accumulated vacation or sick time for which you would have been paid upon leaving anyway), you will most likely be required to pay this back, as well as any health care benefits. Human resources experts say, however, that recouping these costs treads on some sticky issues in employment

Daddy Day Care

The 2000 U.S. Census records that 65 percent of children under age 5 are cared for at home by a parent. Of these, 13 percent are in the primary care of their dads. With increasing numbers of women in the workplace, 40 percent of them making as much as or more than their husbands or partners, it seems fitting that there is a corresponding rise in the number of stay-at-home-dads (SAHD). The At-Home-Dad Network (see Appendix I on page 250) reports that in 2002 there were approximately 2 million men raising kids at home.

This includes men like Charles, 53, who is on his second round as a SAHD. When his first child was born in 1975, Charles was an English professor between jobs, so he did freelance editing from home until his daughter was old enough for kindergarten while his wife brought home the paycheck and benefits. After a remarriage and a second career in banking, he took early retirement, and now he's happily back home caring for his infant son while his wife continues her career as a literary agent.

law, so most employers don't actually go this far. Their advice? Just to be on the safe side, go back to work for a few weeks or a month before handing in your notice. The same goes if you decide to be a stay-at-home mother after your leave ends.

NICE WORK IF YOU CAN GET IT

You've now come full circle, from working, to working while pregnant, to being on leave, to becoming a mother, to (mostly likely) going back to work. Welcome to the ranks of working mothers all over the world, and the challenges—and delights—of being in this position.

Chances are, you'll find yourself in the same position Lindi, a 37-year-old real estate broker, was in. As she complained one day to her husband about the numerous projects she had at work, the list of things she wanted to do with her two small children, her worries about managing an upcoming vacation, and her need to get the dog to his veterinary appointment, finish the book she was reading for book group, and volunteer at the community center, her husband gently interrupted. "Hon," he said, "your only problem is that your life is too full of good things." She paused, and chuckled, blushing. "Yeah," she said, "you're right."

Your life, too, is probably fuller now than it ever has been. But you've survived—you balanced pregnancy and work. You have your baby, and you're making it through the transition back into the workplace, weighing your options and making some of the most difficult choices you've ever made. Now on to the next stage of your life—balancing motherhood and work.

KEYS TO KEEPING THE BALANCE

Almost two-thirds of women who take family leave after a birth or adoption return to work, typically after about 10 weeks. Of these, significant numbers go back to work but make changes in their work arrangements, participating in part-time, job sharing, or flextime options, telecommuting, or working from home for themselves or someone else.

You can provide an infant with the benefits of breastfeeding after you return to work by establishing a plentiful milk supply prior to your return, nursing when you're home, and expressing milk at work for your baby's use at day care.

Thirteen percent of infants cared for in their own homes by a parent are cared for by their fathers.

Women returning to work after having a baby often benefit from redefining workplace success in terms of goals met and tasks accomplished, rather than number of hours worked.

Employers and employees both reap the benefits of family-friendly working arrangements. With such arrangements, employees stay happy and committed, and employers enjoy lower employee absenteeism and greater employee retention.

THE BALANCING ACT

Sigmund Freud, the father of psychoanalysis, was once asked to describe the formula for a happy life. "Lieben und arbeiten," he replied sagely. "Love and work."

Now, note that Freud didn't say that these two things had to come in equal proportions at all times. Ultimately, when we talk about achieving a balance between work and family we are talking, well, baloney. For most of us, there's simply no contest. Our children, our families, are the most important things in our lives. If we love our jobs, if we're passionate about and committed to what we do, we are indeed fortunate; but when it comes to balancing, the scales almost invariably tip in favor of our kids and our partners.

Thus, a more realistic notion of balance implies achieving some sort of stable relationship between the important elements in our lives. You can hold two things steady even if you hold one of them higher than the other.

THE NEXT STEPS: BECOMING A FAMILY

You've made it—or you will. You've figured out how to balance your work and your pregnancy and come out on the other side with a job, and—hallelujah!—a baby. Now you sit in the dark in the middle of the night and nestle and feed your child and feel amazed, exhausted and content. But every so often, a little voice in your head says, hmmm, a baby and a job—now what? That's when you may have a little moment of panic and realize you've signed on for the long haul.

Much of the first year of your child's life will be spent getting to know one another. Hopefully, during those early days and weeks together, you and your partner have established a sense of rhythm and reciprocal communication.

Once upon a time this was called "bonding," and it was thought of as a one-time event that took place shortly after birth. The practice of "rooming in" with your baby in the hospital after delivery comes from this instant bonding concept, the idea that mom and baby need to be together as much as possible from the very first moment of birth in order to fall in love.

Today we know that, rather than the lightning bolt from the blue joining mother and baby together instantly, it can take days or even weeks—and thousands of small interactions with both parent and baby contributing equally and deliberately to what pediatrician and parenting guru T. Berry Brazelton calls "the baby dance"—before you become attuned to your baby's rhythms, behavioral cues, and vocalizations.

So, for instance, when the baby cries, you respond by offering comfort. When baby laughs, you respond by laughing delightedly right back at her, or with a gentle touch or tickle, or a softly excited word of praise. Your baby learns that your behaviors are not random, but are connected in meaningful, predictable ways to her own. Over time, there grows a strong and dependable form of communication between you and your baby, your husband and your baby, your caregiver and your baby.

This all results in attachment, an emotional bond and sense of security and love that a child who experiences consistent and stable caregiving develops with the people who care for and love him. This kind of security enables a child to trust that his needs will be met. Children who are said to be securely attached are more likely, for instance, to explore their environment without undue fear, returning to you for an emotional refueling—a quick cuddle, a kiss, or just a moment of nearness—before setting off again to learn about this brave new world.

Although there is a great deal of emphasis these days on enhancing a young child's cognitive development—which many parents believe is the best way to plan ahead for future school successes—the best foundation for strong cognitive development is sound emotional development. A baby thus nurtured is able to trust and derive security and warmth from her caregivers, which in turn enables her to go about the business of learning about her environment. She may occasionally return to or look back at her mother for reassurance. But for the most part, because she has love, she is ready for work.

What does this mean for your continued ability to balance work and parenting? For one thing, a comfortably attached child—though at first it may sound counterintuitive—is a child who will fare better in day care (assuming the day care is of reasonably high quality) than a child whose attachment to his parents is less than secure. A securely attached child quickly gets the idea: Mom will be back after work. Though he may give you the cold shoulder for a few minutes when you return, he's only bestowing upon you the strong emotions he's saved up for you all day. You're the one he trusts with them, and you're the one who will soon be able to comfort him at the end of a good but tiring day. A securely attached child, particularly one with a sensitive and responsive caregiver, also understands that, just as his world is stable and predictable with his family, his needs will similarly be met by his day care provider. And when you know that your child is happy and well cared for, it enables you to be a better, more productive, and happier worker.

NEGOTIATING FOR TWO

After you bring your baby home, you will most likely feel like you're now attached to a rather short tether. Of course, you are bound body and soul to your child, metaphorically speaking, but there is more than a grain of literal truth to it. If you're home alone with the baby most days, you may feel this very keenly. You take 5-minute showers, listening for the sound of wails coming from the playpen you have put right next to the bathroom door. When your husband is home on a Saturday, you run out for no more than an hour or two to meet a girlfriend, have lunch, or visit the library to see whether you can still read after losing all that amniotic fluid. The truth of this new kind of closeness is reflected in the way we often talk about our little ones: We're not just close, we're joined at the hip, on a short leash. The baby is the King of Cling, a velcro monkey, your little stick-tight.

Would most of us have it any other way? Probably not. This is the kind of closeness we were hoping for in the first place.

At the same time, though, motherhood is very freeing. Being the protector of such a fantastic little being brings out the bravery in most of us. We'd fight lions and tigers and Senate subcommittees seeking to revoke healthcare funding, all for the sake of our children. Those of us who can now laugh in the face of danger may also find that we've become fearless negotiators, single-minded advocates for ourselves and for our families.

What happens to you at work affects not only how you feel about your job, but your life at home as well. The Families and Work Institute's 1997 National Study of the Changing Workforce found that workplaces ranked as family-friendly and supportive were more likely than other companies to have employees who are satisfied with their jobs, loyal to their employer, and committed to the success of their company. Satisfied, committed employees are also more likely to remain with their employers. On the flip side, employees with less

10 Survival Tips for Working Moms

1. Take care of yourself. Mentally, physically, emotionally. The best thing you can do for your baby's well-being is to take care of yourself.

2. Take care of your relationships. It's a basic women's magazine cliché, but it's really true that making your relationship with your husband or partner your second priority after taking care of yourself ultimately benefits your children.

3. Involve your partner in child care. Then stand back and let him do it, without criticizing if he doesn't do it the same way you would.

4. Value your skills and treat yourself like a professional. Know what benefits and arrangements would make you a better worker and don't be afraid to negotiate for them.

5. Treat your child care provider professionally and with respect.

6. Learn to say yes. Yes to takeout food *again* if you'd rather spend time playing with the baby and your partner than cooking, yes to anyone who offers to help you out at home or at work, yes to any opportunity to explore a more rewarding job, yes to anything that makes your life easier or richer.

7. Learn to say no. No to the people who ask you to volunteer for the church rummage sale during your precious weeks of family leave time, no to the supervisor who asks you to come back to work earlier than you'd planned because it's easier for her—even though the very idea makes you cry, no to anyone who tries to make you feel guilty for being an employed mom.

8. Be flexible. Roll with the punches.

9. Flock together with other moms who share your concerns. Even though the scheduling can get a little tricky for women who work outside the home, try to find yourself a playgroup or mom's group that meets regularly to share the joys and frustrations of working motherhood. Bring your babies or don't, depending on what works best for you, but never underestimate—or be without—the love and power of friendships with others in your situation.

10. Trust yourself. Your mother, grandmother, boss, best friend, and the woman with whom you job share are full of useful advice. But in the end, you have to listen to your heart and do what's best for you, your baby, and your family.

faith in their employer's commitment to a healthy work/life balance experienced (not surprisingly) greater stress, a diminished ability to cope with both work and family crises, and a decline in energy at home. Employees of companies that weren't family-friendly also reported it was more difficult to keep work and home life separate.

The same survey found that more employers are starting to understand the connections among work, home life, employee satisfaction, and their own bottom line, which is invariably strengthened by improved employee morale, productivity, and retention. Keeping a good employee is usually less expensive than hiring and training a new one. Yet, while more than half the U.S. workforce wishes for more flexible working conditions, just 30 percent has them, according to the New York-based Families and Work Institute.

Learning how to negotiate for such benefits in your company once you return from your leave is an ongoing process. You can apply what you've already learned in this book about developing a flexible family leave to your efforts toward developing a flexible work schedule after your return. You might also want to consult WorkOptions.com, which is an Internet resource for employees who need a little technical and moral support before they can approach their employer about making family-friendly changes to the framework of their job.

Finally, there are some jobs that simply can't be made more family friendly. Perhaps daily face time is required with clients or your unique set of skills makes job-sharing an impossibility. If so, you might benefit from investigating other work options. Increasingly, there are numerous resources available to employees who want to step off the beaten path and chart their own. The Third Path Institute of Philadelphia (www.thirdpath.org), for instance, works with families and other groups all over the United States to help them develop creative new arrangements for balancing work and family. Remember, every person who strives for more family-friendly working conditions makes it easier for the next person. Don't be afraid to be a pioneer.

A WELL-BALANCED FAMILY

If this is your first child, you probably can't imagine as you gaze adoringly at your sweet babe, who thrives on little more than love and milk, that in a few years you'll be making yourself crazy wondering whether he's getting enough of the right nutrients. "He hasn't had a vegetable in 3 days," you'll think to yourself. Or "Last week he drank milk like it was going out of style, and this week he won't touch it—he's probably going to get rickets!" And then, invariably, you will wonder whose idea it was to give *you* responsibility for another human being: "What kind of mother *am* I?" you will wonder.

But after a while you'll realize that it isn't about nutritional micromanagement. It doesn't matter that he won't touch broccoli, that he thinks meat is "yucky," that he steadfastly refuses milk. It's okay, because he eats peas like they're candy, he hasn't figured out yet that his favorite chicken *is* meat, and he loves cheese and yogurt. Finally it dawns on you that, if you don't get too hung up on what happens in any 24-hour period, his diet *is*, in the long run, balanced.

Similarly, as a mother, wife or partner, and employee, you will have wonderful, golden days when everything falls into place and everybody's happy, as well as long stretches when it feels like everything and everyone gets short shrift. Work demands and family demands *will* fall out of balance; you can count on it. For weeks, no one gets a decent meal while you finish a project at work. For a month, a string of viruses, ear infections, teething, and rashes saps your strength, your energy, and your tolerance for work. "What kind of mother am I?" you ask yourself *again*.

Then one day you look back and realize you're not doing so badly. You're managing (most days) to keep it all together. You're still employed, your baby is thriving, and no one in your family is clinically malnourished or wearing burlap sacks. Most important: Your baby adores you. *That's* what kind of mother you are.

KEYS TO KEEPING THE BALANCE

✗ After you successfully manage to get through your pregnancy with a job, a baby, and your wits mostly intact, you're on the way to doing the same thing as a mother on the job.

✗ "Balance" is sometimes an illusion; it's just the way we talk about keeping the relationships among the different demands and rewards of life in some kind of stable arrangement. Your family will always be more important than anything else.

✗ The weeks or months you were able to spend at home with your baby pay off in terms of her feeling secure in your family. Securely attached babies are more willing to explore the world around them with you as a safe home base.

✗ Many resources are available for helping you to explore work arrangements that will let you build on this foundation by making choices in your job and in your family life that will keep things in balance.

APPENDICES

Appendix A:
General Information on Pregnancy and Working

BOOKS

Curtis, Glade B., and Judith Schuler. *Your Pregnancy Week by Week*. Perseus, 2000.

Douglas, Ann. *The Mother of All Pregnancy Books*. John Wiley and Sons, 2002.

Lamott, Anne. *Operating Instructions: A Journal of My Son's First Year*. Fawcett, 1994.

Murkoff, Heidi, Arlene Eisenbert, and Sandee Hathaway. *What to Expect When You're Expecting*. Workman Publishing, 2002.

INTERNET RESOURCES

www.babycenter.com
www.ePregnancy.com
www.iParenting.com
www.parentsplace.com

The following sites offer due date calculators:

www.4woman.gov/pregnancy/duedate1.cfm
www.motherhood.com/tools/duedate.asp
www.parentsplace.com/pregnancy/calculator/

Appendix B:
Family and Medical Leave Resources

INTERNET RESOURCES ON NATIONAL LEGISLATION

www.dol.gov

U.S. Department of Labor: Complete text of FMLA regulations

www.dol.gov/wb/welcome.html

U. S. Department of Labor Women's Bureau: Information, statistics, and help with child care, FMLA, women's workplace rights, and fair employment practices

www.9to5.org

Nine to Five: National Association of Working Women: A grassroots organization offering job survival tips, rights information, FMLA information, and help with issues related to fair pay, labor practices, and other topics

www.catalystwomen.org

Catalyst: Nonprofit organization tracking women's work issues and work/family issues. Fact sheets, research, publications, speakers.

www.nationalpartnership.org

National Partnership for Women and Families: Frequently updated information about issues of relevance to working women and their families, including updates of each states' family leave regulations.

ADDITIONAL FAMILY LEAVE BENEFITS BY STATE

The following information was current when the book went to press. Updates to this list can be checked at National Partnership's web site: **www.nationalpartnership.org**.

＊ California: Coverage extends to workplaces with five or more employees; no restrictions on number of hours or months worked. Leave based on time you're considered to be medically disabled, up to 4 months.

* Connecticut: Coverage of workplaces with three or more employees.

* District of Columbia: Coverage of workplaces with 20 or more employees; may take up to 16 weeks every 2 years for childbirth or adoption.

* Hawaii: All working women are covered; employees may collect 58 percent of their wages during leave, which is disability-based and may be extended up to 26 weeks.

* Iowa: Coverage extends to workplaces with at least four employees.

* Kansas: Coverage extends to workplaces with at least four employees.

* Kentucky: Coverage for adoptions of children up to age 7.

* Louisiana: Workplaces with 26 or more employees are covered.

* Maine: Workplaces with 25 or more employees are covered.

* Massachusetts: Workplaces with at least six employees are covered; the employee must have completed the employer's initial probationary period or 3 months of full-time work. Leaves for adoptions of children up to 18 (or disabled individuals up to 23) are included.

* Minnesota: Coverage for employers of 21 or more employees.

* Montana: All working women and adopting parents are covered.

* New Hampshire: Coverage for women at workplaces with at least 6 employees. Nonprofit, educational, and charitable organizations are exempt.

* New Jersey: Women may collect approximately two-thirds of their average weekly wage, up to $401 per week, for 4 weeks prior to the birth and 6 weeks afterward (8 if you have a cesarean-section). Women at workplaces not covered by FMLA have no guarantee of job protection, but still qualify for the partial income replacement.

* New York: Women in non-government jobs employed by both FMLA- and non-FMLA-covered companies collect up to half of their average weekly wage up to $170 per week.

* Oregon: Workplaces with at least 25 employees are covered, as are temporary workers hired for 6 months or more.

* Puerto Rico: All working women are covered, and may be eligible for 50 percent income replacement for up to 8 weeks.

* Rhode Island: All women may be eligible for wage replacement at 50 percent of their average weekly wage (up to $504 per week); women with other children may qualify for a $10 supplement for each additional child (maximum of five). Women not covered by FMLA have no guarantee of job protection but still qualify for income replacement.

* Vermont: Workplaces with 10 or more employees are covered.

* Washington: Workplaces with eight or more employees are covered.

Appendix C: Budget Worksheets

Part I: Monthly Income

	Before Leave	During Leave
From employment	_____	_____
From investments	_____	_____
From rental properties	_____	_____
From all other sources	_____	_____
Total	_____	_____

Part II: Monthly Expenses

	Current Cost	Cost During Family Leave
Rent or mortgage	_____	_____
Utilities	_____	_____
Groceries	_____	_____
Meals out	_____	_____
Car payments	_____	_____
Cars: gas and maintenance	_____	_____
Other transportation	_____	_____
Clothing	_____	_____
Childcare	_____	_____
Tuition payments	_____	_____
Credit card payments	_____	_____
Insurance payments	_____	_____
Other health expenses	_____	_____
Gym memberships	_____	_____
Entertainment	_____	_____
Home/lawn maintenance	_____	_____
Charitable donations	_____	_____

Other expenses	Current Cost	Cost During Family Leave
_____	_____	_____
_____	_____	_____
_____	_____	_____
_____	_____	_____
Total:	_____	_____

Part III: Baby Expenses

Nursery preparation	_____
Baby furniture	_____
Car seat, stroller	_____
Clothing	_____
Child care	_____
Diapers or diaper service	_____
Medical expenses	_____
Breastfeeding supplies; formula	_____
Total:	_____

Appendix D: Pregnancy Symptoms

Neither this list nor the resources on it are intended to be a substitute for professional medical care, but are intended only as a guide. Please seek care from a qualified medical practitioner before making decisions that could affect the health of you and your baby.

BOOKS

Douglas, Ann. *Trying Again: A Guide to Pregnancy After Miscarriage, Stillbirth, and Infant Loss.* Taylor Publishing, 2000.

Friedman, Lynn, and Irene Daria. *Miscarriage: A Woman Doctor's Guide.* Kensington, 2001.

Miller, Olivia H., and Diane Philos Jensen. *Prenatal Yoga Deck: 50 Poses and Meditations.* Chronicle, 2003.

Rich, Laurie A. *When Pregnancy Isn't Perfect: A Layperson's Guide to Complications in Pregnancy.* Larata Press, 1996.

Tracy, Amy E., and Richard H. Schwarz. *The Pregnancy Bed Rest Book: A Survival Guide for Expectant Mothers and Their Families.* Berkley, 2001.

INTERNET RESOURCES

www.acog.com
American College of Obstetricians and Gynecologists Resource Center: Health information for women; resource and referral service for those seeking an ACOG-certified health care provider

www.ahrq.gov
Agency for Healthcare Research and Quality (AHRQ): Smoking cessation support for mothers and others

www.diabetes.org

American Diabetes Association: Information and support for those with gestational diabetes, or those who had diabetes before becoming pregnant

www.mayoclinic.com

Mayo Clinic: General medical resources

www.sidelines.org

Sidelines: Resources for women on bedrest

www.webmd.com

WebMD: General medical resources

Appendix E: Mama Style

BOOKS

Gore, Ariel. *The Hip Mama Survival Guide: Advice from the Trenches on Pregnancy, Childbirth, Cool Names, Clueless Doctors, Potty Training, and Toddler Avengers.* Hyperion, 1998.

Lange, Liz. *Liz Lange's Maternity Style.* Clarkson N. Potter, 2003.

Salmonsahn, Karen. *Hot Mama: How to Have a Babe and Be a Babe.* Chronicle Books, 2003.

Sara, Lauren, and Michel Amaud. *Expecting Style.* Bulfinch Press, 2003.

Serota, Cherie, and Jody Kozlow Gardner. *Pregnancy Chic: The Fashion Survival Guide.* Villard, 1998.

INTERNET RESOURCES

www.onehotmama.com

One Hot Mama: Comprehensive advice and message boards regarding pregnancy style

Online Sources of Pregnancy Wear

Company	Web Site Address	Specialty
Anna Cris	annacris.com	
Assortment of stores	maternitymall.com	
Baby Becoming	babybecoming.com	Plus size maternity clothing
Baby Style	babystyle.com	
Bella Materna	bellamaterna.com	Underclothes and lingerie
Belly Basics	bellybasics.com	Emphasis on clothes for now and after the pregnancy
Bloom'n	bloom-n.com	Will tailor your favorite clothes so you can wear them while pregnant

Company	Web Site Address	Specialty
Cadeau Designs Maternity	cadeaudesigns.com	Includes classy, conservative selections
Expecting in Style	expectinginstyle.com	Includes evening and swimwear
Fit Maternity & Beyond	fitmaternity.com	Workout wear
Gap Maternity	gap.com	
Japanese Weekend	japaneseweekend.com	
J.C. Penney Maternity	jcpenney.com	Includes petite, tall, and plus sizes
Liz Lange Maternity Wear	target.com	
Medela Maternity	medela.com	Specializing in underwear and support garments
Motherhood Maternity	motherhood.com	
Mothers in Motion	mothersinmotion.com	Maternity exercise wear
Motherwear	motherwear.com	Comprehensive site for maternity wear
Naissance on Melrose	naissancematernity.com	
Nicole Michelle Maternity	nicolematernity.com	Includes wedding gowns!
Old Navy Maternity	oldnavy.com	
One Hot Mama	onehotmama.com	Clothes and style advice
The Power of Two	poweroftwo.net	Includes workout wear

Appendix F: Child Care Resources

BOOKS

Choosing Quality Child Care: The American Red Cross Search Guide, 2001.

Hall, Nancy, and Peggy Schmidt. *Goodbyes: How to Say "See You Later" to Your Little Alligator.* Pocket, 1996.

Harms, Thelma. *Infant/Toddler Environment Rating Scale.* Teachers College Press, 1990.

Holcomb, Betty. *Not Guilty! The Good News for Working Mothers.* Touchstone, 2000.

Mason, Linda. *The Working Mother's Guide to Life.* Three Rivers Press, 2003.

INTERNET RESOURCES

www.childcarerr.org

National Association of Child Care Resource and Referral Agencies: Comprehensive information resource for child care providers, families, and communities

www.nafcc.com

National Association for Family Child Care: Referrals for accredited family child care providers and support for family child care providers and their client families

The following sites offer legal advice related to the employment of child care providers:

www.nolo.com
www.immigration.gov

The following sites offer child care provider tax calculators:

www.4homehelp.com/ChildFAQ.html
www.smartmoney.com

Appendix G: Breastfeeding and Work

BOOKS

The American Academy of Pediatrics New Mother's Guide to Breastfeeding. American Academy of Pediatrics, 2002.

Martins, Claire. *The Nursing Mother's Problem Solver.* Fireside, 2000.

Pryor, Gale. *Nursing Mother, Working Mother: The Emotional Guide for Breastfeeding and Staying Close to Your Baby After You Return to Work.* Harvard Common Press, 1997.

Rosenthal, M. Sara, and Gillian Arsenault. *The Breastfeeding Sourcebook.* McGraw-Hill, 2000.

INTERNET RESOURCES

www.ameda.com
Ameda: Includes breastfeeding support products, pumps, bottles, and breastfeeding advice and information

www.aventbaby.com
Avent: Distributor of Avent supplies and products for both bottle- and breastfeeding moms, including pumps, breast pads, and skin care products for mothers and babies

www.Lalecheleague.org
La Leche League: support for breastfeeding moms, medical resources related to breastfeeding, information about laws and policies related to breastfeeding, information about local La Leche League chapters

www.medela.com
Medela: Distributors of Medela products and supplies to support moms who breastfeed, including breast pumps, maternity and nursing wear, and bottles and breast pump carriers; also includes breastfeeding information and advice

Appendix H:
Alternative Work Options
and Work/Life Issues

BOOKS

Anderson, Sandy. *The Work at Home Balancing Act: The Professional Resource Guide for Managing Yourself, Your Work, and Your Family at Home.* Paperback Press, 1998.

Beck, Martha. *Finding Your Own North Star: Claiming the Life You Were Meant to Live.* Three Rivers Press, 2002.

Dinnocenzo, Debra A. *101 Tips for Telecommuters.* Berrett-Koehler, 1999.

Edwards, Paul, Sarah Edwards, and Peter Economy. *Home-Based Business for Dummies.* Dummies, 2000.

Froggatt, Cynthia.*Work Naked: Eight Essential Principles for Peak Performance in the Virtual Workplace.* John Wiley and Sons, 2002.

Leonsky, Rieva. *Start Your Own Business: The Only Start Up Book You'll Ever Need.* Entrepreneur Media, 2001.

Mason, Linda.*The Working Mother's Guide to Life.* Three Rivers Press, 2003.

McDonald, Kathy, and Beth Sirull. *Creating Your Life Collage—Strategies for Solving the Work/Life Dilemma.* Three Rivers Press, 2000.

Miller, Lee E., and Jessica Miller. *A Woman's Guide to Successful Negotiating.* McGraw-Hill, 2002.

Paulson, Edward. *The Complete Idiot's Guide to Starting Your Own Business.* Alpha, 2000.

Zbar, Jeffrey D. *Teleworking and Telecommuting.* Made E–Z, 2002.

Zetlin, Minda. *Telecommuting for Dummies.* Hungry Minds, 2001.

Books from the Families and Work Institute (available at www.familiesandwork.org):
The Corporate Reference Guide to Work-Family Programs
The Family-Friendly Employer: Examples from Europe

Books from The Third Path Institute (available at www.thirdpath.org):
"Shared Care" brochure
Work/Family Options Workbook
Shared Care Guide

INTERNET RESOURCES

See also the Internet resources listed in Appendix B.

www.att.com/telework/get_started/gs_telemp.html
AT&T Telework site: Information on whether you'd be a good candidate for a telecommuting position, whether such an arrangement would meet the needs of your company, and material on how to get started

www.sba.gov/womeninbusiness/wbcs.html
Small Business Administration: Federal government office with information for women wishing to start their own business

www.telecommuting.about.com
About.com: General information on working away from your office

www.workingfromanywhere.com
The International Telwork Association and Council: General

resource for telecommuters and those who wish to investigate distance working options

www.WorkOptions.com

Work Options: Information about designing and negotiating for a non-traditional work arrangement; downloadable templates to purchase to help you investigate, negotiate for, and contract for such a position

Appendix I:
Resources for Fathers

BOOKS

Brott, Armin A. *The Expectant Father: Facts, Tips, and Advice for Dads-to-Be.* Abbeville Press, 2001.

Gill, Libby. *Stay-at-Home Dads: The Essential Guide to Creating the New Family.* Plume, 2001.

Levine, James A., and Todd L. Pittinsky. *Working Fathers: New Strategies for Balancing Work and Families.* Perseus, 1997.

Pruett, Kyle D. *Fatherneed: Why Father Care Is As Essential As Mother Care for Your Child.* Broadway Books, 2001.

INTERNET RESOURCES

www.athomedad.com

At Home Dad: Offers general advice for fathers who are their child's primary caregiver; started by a stay-at-home father

www.dadstoday.com

Dads Today: A spin-off of iParenting.com, with message boards, child development information, and other support geared toward dads

www.fatherhoodproject.org

The Fatherhood Project: This national research and education project mounts efforts designed to bust stereotypes of dads who stay home with their kids, conducts research into strategies for creating dad-supportive workplaces, and works with state governments to foster responsible fatherhood.

www.fathers.com

The National Center for Fathering: A nonprofit institute devoted to research on and support for fathers

www.slowlane.com

Slowlane: Offers general advice and support for stay-at-home dads, primary caregiving fathers, and their families; helps men connect with other stay-at-home dads in their local area

INDEX

D

E